Enrichment Magazine

IN THIS ISSUE . . .

To the Director

This student folder contains nine study leaflets and the enrichment magazine. Remove the center staple and distribute the leaflets as indicated in the leaders guide. This magazine should be distributed at the first session for use throughout the course.

3558 S. Jefferson Ave., St. Louis, MO 63118-3968

1-800-325-3040 • www.cph.org

Written by Reed Lessing
Edited by Brian Chisamore

Cover illustration The Prophet Zechariah, Sistine Chapel, Erich Lessing/Art Resource, NY

Graphic design by Tamara Bishop

This publication may be available in braille, in large print, or on cassette tape for the visually impaired. Please allow 8 to 12 weeks for delivery. Write to Lutheran Braille Workers, P.O. Box 5000, Yucaipa, CA 92399; call toll-free 1-800-925-6092; or visit the Web site: www.LBWinc.org.

Manufactured in the United States of America

1 2 3 4 5 6 7 8 9 10   22 21 20 19 18 17 16 15 14 13

BURIED ALIVE!

Buried!

In an old *Alfred Hitchcock Presents* episode, a woman prisoner becomes good friends with the prison caretaker. When a prisoner died, he would ring the bell, get the body, put it in a casket, and nail it shut. Then, placing the casket on a wagon, he would take it to the graveyard outside the prison walls and bury the corpse.

Knowing this routine, the woman convict devised an escape plan and shared it with the caretaker. "The next time the bell rings," she said, "I'll leave my prison cell and sneak into the coffin with the dead body. Nail the lid shut, then take the coffin outside the prison with me in it. Bury the coffin," she continued, "and because there will be enough air for me to breathe for some time, you can come back to the graveyard under the cover of night, dig up the coffin, and set me free."

The caretaker agreed to the plan.

One day, the woman prisoner hears the ringing of the death bell. She gets up, sneaks down the hallway, finds the coffin containing the dead body, and climbs in. Soon she hears the pounding of hammer and nails. The coffin is lifted onto the wagon and taken outside to the graveyard. After the last dirt is poured on the coffin, she begins to giggle out loud, "I'm free, free!"

Feeling curious, she lights a match to identify the prisoner beside her—and in the glimmer of light, she discovers that she is lying next to the dead caretaker! In classic Alfred Hitchcock fashion, this final scene fades as we hear the woman screaming and screaming, then silence.

Have you been buried like that before? Sure you have, and so have I.

Buried under Everything

We've been buried in questions: "If God is so good, why do I hurt so bad?" "If Jesus is the light, why am I in the dark?"

We've been buried in disappointment: "You're not like your older brother!" "You're just not like our last pastor!"

We've been buried in responsibilities: "Here is a thirty-page case study. Be ready to discuss it tomorrow." "Honey, the kids have softball and baseball games tomorrow."

We've been buried in the past ever since the minute we lost our temper, the hour we lost our purity, the day we lost control, and the years we lost our priorities. And on top of it all, we're buried in our daily self-righteousness, self-satisfaction, self-sufficiency, and self-will.

It's dark, tight, and claustrophobic. The enemy has nailed the lid shut. And if there isn't screaming, we all know about heavy sighs, lifeless looks, and empty hearts.

Haggai knows the same sinking feelings all too well.

The Jerusalem temple was still a fire-blackened pile of rubble (2 Kings 25:9). The ark of the covenant with its Mercy Seat and cherubim was gone forever; the tablets of the Ten Commandments, the manna, and Aaron's rod had been swept away, as had the Urim and Thummim and the eternal fire on the altar. In 587 BC, the year Babylon destroyed Judah and Jerusalem, everything was gone with the wind.

To be sure, some of the movers and shakers in the community were living comfortably in "paneled houses" (Haggai 1:4), but most of the people were enduring poverty, scarcity, and hopelessness. Drought had brought with it crop failure, leading to inflation and acute hunger. Haggai summarizes this sorry state of affairs by depicting a person earning his wages, only to put the money in a purse full of holes (v. 6). Life was now dictated by famine, fate, and foreign oppression. Where was God?

© Vika Valter / iStockphoto.com

The date, "the second year of Darius the king, in the sixth month, on the first day of the month" (v. 1), corresponds to August 29, 520 BC. It is one of four dates listed in the book, the last one being equivalent to December 18, 520 BC. Though Haggai's ministry only lasted a little more than three months, he is mentioned with Zechariah in Ezra's account of building the second temple (Ezra 5:1; 6:14).

Although Cyrus II, the first king of the new Persian empire, permitted those in exile to return to Judah and authorized the reconstruction of the temple in Jerusalem, the efforts stalled because of opposition and apathy. It wasn't difficult to delay construction of the temple. Judah had been devastated by the Babylonians; people needed to devote their time and energy to the task of sheer survival. Who had time to worry about religion? People were buried in what seemed to be never-ending pain.

Yet in the midst of all the darkness, the Lord makes a great promise to Zerubbabel, the community's governor: "I will take you, O Zerubbabel My servant, the son of Shealtiel, declares the Lord, and make you like a signet ring" (Haggai 2:23).

What is a signet ring? In ancient times, a king or a noble would wear a ring that acted as a stamp. When issuing decrees, commandments, and resolutions, the king would seal the scroll with clay or wax with the royal signet or emblem authenticating the message. How does this relate to Zerubbabel and Haggai's community? In this descendant of David (Matthew 1), the Lord's presence is authenticated. He will not abandon His people in the pit of their despair!

There is One greater than Zerubbabel who certifies God's reality. He is also of the house and lineage of David. His name is *Jesus*. And Jesus is our hope when we feel buried, boxed in, and forever stuck.

Our Unfailing Hope

Why?

Jesus allowed the enemy to marshal every weapon of mass destruction. Satan gathered Judas, Pilate, and Herod. He assembled thorns, three nails, and a spear. Then there was screaming and more screaming on a Friday we call "good."

It all ended in total silence. Jesus was crucified, dead, and was *buried*. Nothing is as bottomless as a pit, as lifeless as a grave, as hopeless as a tomb. Smell the mildew, the odor of blood, and the stench of death. See the confines, the darkness, and the sealed stone.

But how could death hold Jesus? He is the Father's authenticating presence in the world. Here is God's signet ring stamping "VICTORY" upon your life and mine! And He does it to us through Holy Baptism.

Buried and Raised

Unlike the woman prisoner in the Alfred Hitchcock show, we are not literally buried in the ground. Nevertheless, we certainly are buried, and buried under so much—under our troubles, grief, and regrets.

There is another difference between us and the woman in the show. Unlike her, we are not buried with a dead corpse. Instead, you and I are buried with a living Jesus who has conquered death and the grave. Paul puts it this way: "We were buried therefore with Him by baptism into death, in order that, just as Christ was raised from the dead by the glory of the Father, we too might walk in newness of life" (Romans 6:4; see also Colossians 2:12). Through the water and Word, we have been buried and raised with Jesus. And so our hopeless screams are forever changed into baptized and Spirit-filled praises to the Lamb!

Portions of this article were adapted from "Buried!" presented on The Lutheran Hour on April 25, 2004. Printed with permission of the International Lutheran Laymen's League.

PERFECT PEACE

My attic is filled with bent, broken, and busted stuff. My son, Jonathan, asked me to fix G.I. Joe's head when our dog Maverick chewed it off. Several years have passed, and Joe is still headless. My daughter Abi asked me to fix her bookshelf. The shelf is still bookless. And my other daughter asked me to repair her bike. Lori is still bikeless.

What is my strategy? Hide all the torn, tattered, and twisted things in the attic. Out of sight, out of mind. And presto! After a few years, the whole family will be clueless.

But there is one slight, tiny problem. Occasionally my children have the audacity to go up into our attic, and then I'm reminded, again, of my inability to be "Mr. Fix-It Dad." And in the presence of their inquisition, I am again speechless! The attic at my home is a testimony to my inability to fix what is broken. And while my family waits for the grand opening of Reed's Restoration and Repair Rotunda, they all feel completely hopeless!

The Old Testament prophet Haggai had the same problem. His life was surrounded by a bunch of broken stuff that he couldn't fix. Haggai describes his mess throughout the first chapter of his book: People have sown much but harvested little. They eat but are never satisfied; they drink but are never content. The people of Judah are cold, in the middle of a drought, and feeling listless and despondent.

Satan is the chief source of this brokenness, for Haggai and for us. His lies strip away the Father's baptismal promises, eucharistic joy, and Gospel power. The devil's temptations destroy marital fidelity, moral responsibility, and churchly civility. His deceptions lead us to whisper wicked words, lunge for lustful looks, hate with hard hearts, and go on in godless gossip. The end result is a cluttered attic that we keep hidden to keep everyone clueless. But it makes us completely hopeless.

Fixing Humpty Dumpty

Throughout the Old Testament, the Lord reveals Himself in concrete ways and promises His real presence in specific places. God's glory filled the tabernacle (Exodus 40:34–38), was enthroned above the ark of the covenant (2 Samuel 6:2), and chose Solomon's temple as His holy habitation (1 Kings 8). In great love, time after time, the Lord rends the heavens and comes to dwell in the midst of His people. Knowing this, Haggai records these words of God: "Go up to the hills and bring wood and build the house, that I may take pleasure in it and that I may be glorified" (Haggai 1:8).

The prophet continues, "The latter glory of this house shall be greater than the former, says the LORD of hosts. And in this place I will give peace, declares the LORD of hosts" (2:9). When the second temple is built, God promises that it will be a place of peace. The Hebrew word translated "peace" is *shalom*. *Shalom* doesn't mean the absence of warfare; rather, it denotes "to restore," "to make right," "to fix." God's gift of *shalom* puts Humpty Dumpty back together again. Haggai pins his hope on this gift of *shalom*.

So did Israel.

For example, in one of his salvation oracles, Isaiah writes "*shalom, shalom*" (Isaiah 26:3). This is often translated "perfect peace." For Isaiah, restoration comes through the Suffering Servant. "The punishment that brings us *shalom* is upon Him, and by His wounds we are healed" (53:5, author's translation).

This points us to the One Isaiah calls "The Prince *Shalom*" (9:6). At Jacob's well, He spoke with a Samaritan woman who had been devastated by men's empty promises. In Jericho, He met Zacchaeus, who had been consumed by the world's fleeting promises. Countless other times, Jesus fixed torn, tattered, and twisted people. His goal was singular: put Humpty Dumpty back together again.

But to do this, our Savior had to be paraded outside of Jerusalem to a place called Golgotha where people were intentionally bent and broken, maimed and mauled, and then systematically thrown away. There Satan stalked Him, took aim, shot straight, and killed.

But on the third day, *the* Temple was rebuilt (John 2:19). And, just as in Haggai's day, from the new Temple comes God's gift of *shalom*. John writes, "On the evening of that day, the first day of the week, the doors being locked where the disciples were for fear of the Jews, Jesus came and stood among them and said to them, 'Peace be with you.' When He had said this, He showed them His hands and His side. Then the disciples were glad when they saw the Lord. Jesus said to them again, 'Peace be with you'" (John 20:19–21). Jesus offers the gift of *double*—and therefore *perfect*—peace! This *shalom* is delivered in concrete ways and in a specific place. At the Lord's Supper we receive the true body and blood of Jesus Christ that completely forgives all of our sins. And this forgiveness begins to put our broken pieces back together again.

In fact, the entire experience at the Communion altar is one of *shalom*. After the consecration of the elements, the pastor says, "The peace of the Lord be with you always." The congregation then sings the Agnus Dei, which includes the words "Lamb of God, You take away the sin of the world; grant us peace" (*LSB*, p. 163). After we taste and see that our Lord is so very good, we often sing the Nunc Dimittis, the "Song of Simeon": "Lord, now You let Your servant go in peace" (p. 165). And then we hear these words from the Aaronic Benediction. *Shalom* is God's final word:

"The Lord bless you and keep you;

the Lord make His face to shine upon you and be gracious to you;

the Lord lift up His countenance upon you and give you *shalom*" (Numbers 6:24–26, author's translation).

"The Lord bless you and keep you;
the Lord make His face to shine upon you and be gracious to you;
the Lord lift up His countenance upon you and give you *shalom*"
Numbers 6:24–26

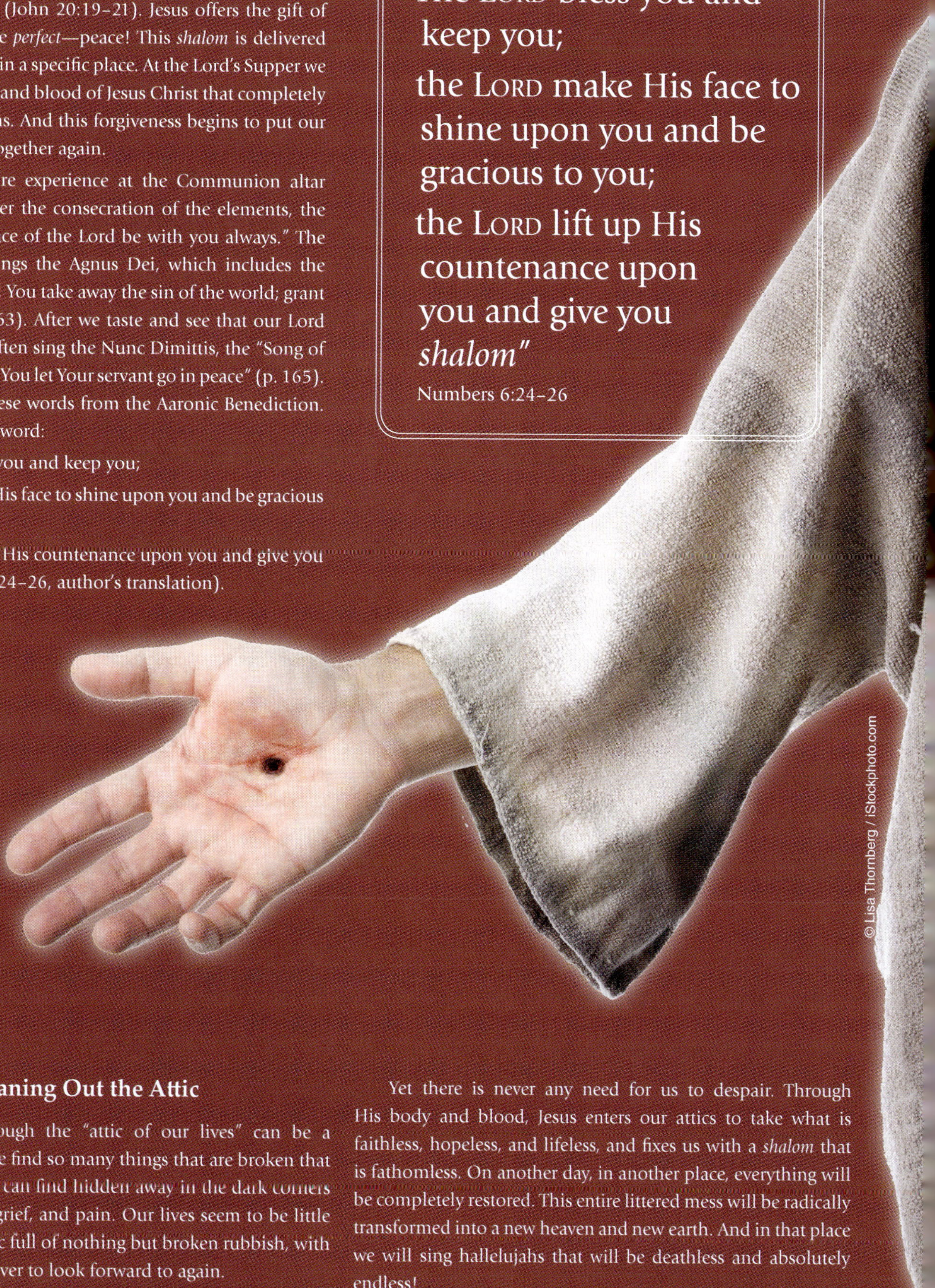

© Lisa Thornberg / iStockphoto.com

Cleaning Out the Attic

Rummaging through the "attic of our lives" can be a distressing activity. We find so many things that are broken that we long to repair. We can find hidden away in the dark corners a lifetime of regrets, grief, and pain. Our lives seem to be little more than an old attic full of nothing but broken rubbish, with nothing good for us ever to look forward to again.

Yet there is never any need for us to despair. Through His body and blood, Jesus enters our attics to take what is faithless, hopeless, and lifeless, and fixes us with a *shalom* that is fathomless. On another day, in another place, everything will be completely restored. This entire littered mess will be radically transformed into a new heaven and new earth. And in that place we will sing hallelujahs that will be deathless and absolutely endless!

© iStockphoto

THE UNSHAKABLE KINGDOM

It was midafternoon in central China on May 12, 2008, when suddenly, all hell broke loose. An earthquake hit with a magnitude of 8.0 on the Richter scale. Concrete panels, crumpled steel, and crushed tile buried tens of thousands of people. They groped in the darkness, gasping for air, wondering how long they would live.

These kinds of life-changing earthquakes are familiar terrain for Haggai. He records these divine words: "And I will shake all nations, so that the treasures of all nations shall come in, and I will fill this house with glory, says the Lord of hosts" (Haggai 2:7). An early Christian translation of this verse, called the Latin Vulgate, reads "the Desire of all nations." But this is not what the Hebrew says. More literally, it reads, "the desired *things* of all nations." In 2 Chronicles 36:10, these are referred to as "the precious vessels of the house of the Lord." Through Haggai, God promises that when He shakes the nations, the liturgical vessels taken by Nebuchadnezzar from Solomon's temple in 587 BC will return to their rightful place.

The prophet goes on to describe another earthquake that will not only shake the nations, but even heaven and earth: "The word of the Lord came a second time to Haggai on the twenty-fourth day of the month, 'Speak to Zerubbabel, governor of Judah, saying, I am about to shake the heavens and the earth, and to overthrow the throne of kingdoms. I am about to destroy the strength of the kingdoms of the nations, and overthrow the chariots and their riders. And the horses and their riders shall go down, every one by the sword of his brother'" (Haggai 2:20–22). When understood in light of the early years of Darius the Persian's reign (522–485 BC), these verses indicate that the Lord will one day overthrow his kingdom. This, in turn, is a portent of God's authority over all the kingdoms in heaven and on earth.

SHAKE, RATTLE, AND ROLL

It would have been easy for Haggai and his community to believe that the Persian Empire was absolute and therefore eternal. Pragmatists perhaps decided to accommodate to the new realities, including the worship of Persian gods and conformity to the religion of the day. After all, Persia was not only a political-military superpower; it was also an advanced, sophisticated, winsome culture. The empire seduced people into its worldview with its military pomp and intellectual and spiritual symbols.

Into this dilemma, Haggai speaks. And he says that the Persian kingdom—indeed, *all* the kingdoms of this world—are temporal and will quickly pass away. The Lord is going to shake, rattle, and roll *everything* so that finally, only His kingdom will stand.

Haggai's vision of God's coming kingdom contains multiple fulfillments. The temple was rebuilt, the walls of Jerusalem were restored, and the worshiping community was reconstituted. But more shaking was on the way. Both John the Baptist and Jesus announce the advent of God's kingdom (Matthew 3:2; 4:17).

© Michal Bryc / iStockphoto.com

After the death and resurrection of Jesus Christ, the Holy Spirit propelled people to live for and proclaim the coming of God's kingdom. On one occasion, this message reached a place called Thessalonica where the Jews attacked Paul and Silas, claiming, "These men . . . have turned the world upside down" (Acts 17:6). The power of the Gospel is an earthshaking, life-changing power! The Jews went on to say, "They are all acting against the decrees of Caesar, saying that there is another king, Jesus" (v. 7). Over the course of history, countless kingdoms, governments, and ideologies have postured themselves as the ultimate authority. However, on the Last Day, every impostor will be exposed. The Father will announce to all that Jesus is the "King of kings" (Revelation 19:16).

Every other kingdom cracks and crumbles. Everything else is temporary and transitory. All other ground is sinking sand!

How do we know for sure?

Listen again, for the first time.

One night, there were a few small tremors. In fact, they were so small, no one even noticed. But the shaking picked up when the treasurer left the room. Within minutes, these ripples increased in their intensity. In staccato-like fashion, earthquakes began to hit: one kiss, three nails, and the next day, six hours of suffering. And then a massive earthquake hit: "And behold, the curtain of the temple was torn in two, from top to bottom. And the earth shook, and the rocks were split" (Matthew 27:51). This was followed by the mother of all earthquakes: "And behold, there was a great earthquake, for an angel of the Lord descended from heaven and came and rolled back the stone and sat on it" (28:2). And then what the angel said unleashed the greatest news the world has ever heard: "He is not here, for He has risen, as He said" (v. 6).

This earthquake changes everything!

THE FINAL EARTHQUAKE

Five days after the massive 2008 Chinese earthquake, a group of rescue workers found the dead body of a young woman. She was in a kneeling position. Her back was hunched over, supporting a crumbled ceiling; her arms stretched forward, her hands thrust firmly into the muddy earth. As the rescue workers walked away, suddenly the team leader understood. He ran back to the woman and reached underneath her body. There, in the tiny shelter that the woman created by using her body as a protective shield, was a baby. He was about three months old, alive, unhurt, and sleeping soundly. Inside the baby's clothing was a cell phone. On it was this message: "My dear baby, remember, I love you."

So often we can become disappointed by this world's passing show. So often we may find that what we thought was lasting and enduring caves in all around us. We may at times see the collapse of things we sincerely believed would always stand.

No matter how earthshaking your times may be, there is something you may always remember: Jesus shelters you, holds you, and protects you. Building upon the words of Haggai, the writer to the Hebrews promises one more earthquake for the ages, when Christ comes again: "At that time His voice shook the earth, but now He has promised, 'Yet once more I will shake not only the earth but also the heavens.' This phrase, 'Yet once more,' indicates the removal of things that are shaken—that is, things that have been made—in order that the things that cannot be shaken may remain" (Hebrews 12:26–27). We have an unshakeable joy and unshakeable courage because we are part of God's unshakeable kingdom. The very gates of hell will never, ever prevail against it! "Therefore let us be grateful for receiving a kingdom that cannot be shaken, and thus let us offer to God acceptable worship, with reverence and awe" (v. 28).

8 VISIONS IN THE NIGHT

Prophets were sometimes called "seers" (1 Samuel 9:9). It is therefore not surprising that references to their visions are prominent in their books. This role is attested to in the words that introduce prophetic books, such as "The book of the vision of Nahum of Elkosh" (Nahum 1:1). Prophetic visions often occur in a series. For example, Ezekiel offers four vision reports; Amos sees five visions; and Jeremiah has two visions as part of his call. The most famous prophetic vision is recorded in Isaiah 6. Here the prophet says, "I saw the Lord, . . . high and lifted up" (Isaiah 6:1). Isaiah goes on to describe flying seraphim, shaking thresholds, billowing smoke, and a live coal taken from an altar that touches his lips.

On February 15, 519 BC, two months after Haggai's final message, God showed Zechariah eight night visions. These eight visions may seem obscure or confusing to us, yet they all lead us to rely on the promised Savior, our Lord Jesus.

The First Vision (Zechariah 1:7–17)

The center of the first vision is a man riding on a red horse who is "the angel of the LORD" (v. 11). Early Christian commentators like Justin Martyr and Eusebius recognized this "angel" to be none other than the Second Person of the Trinity, our Lord Jesus Christ. Francis Pieper, one of our most famous Lutheran theologians, likewise notes that the Angel of the Lord is not just a messenger for God but is God Himself.

And what does this Messenger do? He intercedes for Israel: "O LORD of hosts, how long will You have no mercy on Jerusalem and the cities of Judah, against which You have been angry these seventy years?" (v. 12). Jesus likewise intercedes for the Roman soldiers crucifying Him: "Father, forgive them, for they know not what they do" (Luke 23:34). The Spirit of Jesus also intercedes for us (Romans 8:26–27).

The Second Vision (1:18–21)

In Zechariah's first vision, the Lord expresses His anger over what other nations had been doing to Israel. In the second night vision, God reveals how He will deal with these nations, symbolized by four horns. He will send four craftsmen against His adversaries, and they will execute judgment. The four horns, or the enemy nations, will be met with four craftsmen. For every enemy fighting His people, God raises up counteracting powers to destroy it. Evil will never have the final word in our lives!

The Third Vision (2:1–13)

In his third vision, Zechariah sees a man measuring Jerusalem, a scene that evokes a reference in the first vision (see Zechariah 1:16). The city will have a vast population, and it will be protected by the Lord. The "wall of fire" is much like the pillar of fire that accompanied Israel through the wilderness and separated the Egyptians from the Israelites at the Red Sea. Further, the return of God's glory in the midst of Jerusalem (2:5) recalls the time when the Lord took three steps to leave the temple during the Babylonian crisis of 587 BC (Ezekiel 9:3; 10:19; 11:23). Now He will return. The Lord is present to protect His people, forever!

The "gracious and comforting words" (Zechariah 1:13) of the first three visions promise the following:

- the Lord's overthrow of Gentile powers (1:18–21);
- the restoration of the people of Judah from the Babylonian exile (1:12; 2:4); and
- the future habitation of Jerusalem (2:4).

The Fourth Vision (3:1–10)

Moving to the fourth vision, we are reminded of an ink spot on the wall of the Wartburg Castle. One night, Martin Luther had a dream that Satan appeared to him, reading a long scroll with all of his sins. As the reading of the list proceeded, Luther's terrors grew until finally he jumped up and cried, "It is all true, Satan, and many more sins I have committed in my life which are known to God only; but write at the bottom of your list, 'the blood of Jesus Christ, God's Son, cleanses us from all sin.'" Then, grasping the inkwell on his table, he threw it at the devil.

Zechariah's fourth vision deals with the same problem of sin. The focal point of the vision is in verses 8–9, where God promises to remove Joshua's iniquity. Paul sums this all up for us: "There is therefore now no condemnation for those who are in Christ Jesus" (Romans 8:1).

The Fifth Vision (4:1–14)

While the previous vision considers Joshua the high priest, the fifth one shines the light on Zerubbabel, the governor. The new temple will not be completed by human ingenuity or drive, but by the Spirit of God (v. 6). The people had tried to rebuild its temple by their own strength immediately upon their return from Babylon more than sixteen years earlier, but that turned out to be a failure (Ezra 3:8–13). This instructs us not to rely on our resources, wisdom, or cunning. May we be content to allow the Holy Spirit to call, gather, and enlighten lives through His power and might, knowing that His purpose will be accomplished.

The Sixth (5:1–4) and Seventh (5:5–11) Visions

Visions six and seven are twin messages; the sixth vision reveals that unbelievers will be purged from Israel, while the seventh demonstrates that wickedness itself will be removed. Verses 1–4 warn that individual sinners will be judged, while verses 5–11 promise that the very principle of evil will be abolished from Israel. These prophecies are pointing to the Last Day. When Christ returns, He will hurl Satan and his minions into the lake of fire (Revelation 20:10). Then, forever free of all wickedness and evil, we will sing the song of the Lamb forever and ever!

The Eighth Vision (6:1–15)

The eighth vision mentions for the second time "the man whose name is the Branch" (v. 12). This Branch becomes the book's chief subject, especially in Zechariah 9–14. For example, the prophet writes, "Rejoice greatly, O daughter of Zion! Shout aloud, O daughter of Jerusalem! Behold, your king is coming to you; righteous and having salvation is He, humble and mounted on a donkey, on a colt, the foal of a donkey" (9:9). Again, he says, "So I took the thirty pieces of silver and threw them into the house of the Lord, to the potter" (11:13). And again, "They look on Me, on Him whom they have pierced" (12:10). These prophecies all point to Palm Sunday. They refer to Jesus' triumphal entry into Jerusalem, Judas's betrayal, and our Lord's crucifixion.

Light in the Dark

The series of night visions that Zechariah was given can be difficult or confusing for us. It can be easy for us to read them and not immediately see how they depict God's infinite blessings to us. The visions can seem so dark and obscure.

Yet the light of Christ can shine even through the darkness of our confusion. In all eight of these visions, we are reminded of and pointed to God's grace in Christ. The visions depict for us His compassion for His people, His protection of His Church, His judgment against evil, and the vindication of His elect. These all find their fulfillment in Jesus, who was dead but is now alive forevermore!

JUSTICE For All!

There is so much hardship and tragedy in the world. It can be heartrending to consider all the pain and suffering that people throughout the world and even in our own community are undergoing. Sometimes we can only wonder what can be done or how we can respond. Zechariah responds to all the pain with these words: "Thus says the Lord of hosts: 'Execute true justice'" (Zechariah 7:9 NKJV).

That may seem a little odd to us at first. After all, the picture that the word "justice" brings to mind is that of a blindfolded woman holding a set of balances. "Justice" is often understood as fairness and equality. But Zechariah's justice is different—it is a call to actively protect widows, orphans, immigrants, and the poor (7:10). The prophet's command for justice is a call to marshal resources so that people are housed, fed, clothed, and incorporated into the economic fabric of Israel's community.

The prophetic cry for justice is still relevant for us today. We can even see this same call being made to us by Jesus (see Matthew 23:23; Luke 11:42). Clearly this call to render justice to those around us is a continuing part of the life of the Church in the world.

What does this mean for us?

Life in This Present World

Our Savior gave His disciples one mandate, and that was to make disciples from among all the nations (Matthew 28:18–20). The Great Commission, however, does not mean the Church must ignore the difficult issues facing people. Jesus not only offers the free gift of life after death; He also empowers the baptized for life *before* death. And in this life, we are called to assist the fatherless, the widows, the diseased, and the disenfranchised. We may recall that these were all the people for whom our Lord was so concerned during His earthly ministry. For instance, Jesus gave sight to blind Bartimaeus (Mark 10:46–52); healed the Canaanite woman's sick daughter (Matthew 15:22–28); raised to life Jairus's deceased daughter (Luke 8:41–56); fed the multitudes on two different occasions (Mark 5:44; 8:9); and cured the woman with a flow of blood (vv. 24–34).

But unfortunately, there is a temptation within the Church to separate spiritual issues from political and social concerns. Many Christians believe the word *spiritual* means otherworldly piety. They have been taught that a "spiritual" person is one whose inner eyes are cast heavenward in prayer and contemplation. To be "spiritual" suggests communing with one's heavenly Father by focusing upon the invisible realities and eternal mysteries of His holiness. To live "spiritually" is often thought of in terms of passive detachment from this world, a transcending of the self to a higher, more sublime world. According to this thinking, a "spiritual" person is really only consumed with one agenda: "to win souls for Jesus." All other activity is inferior and lacking in priority.

© iStockphoto.com

But the Bible in general, and the Book of Zechariah in particular, challenges us to renounce this type of thinking. To be sure, assisting the poor, working toward fairer wages, and so on does not in any way save us. Salvation will never be accomplished by means of political achievement. Solving political and social issues brings only provisional order and peace, never eternal order and peace.

However, God has given us a definite moral vision, one that is epitomized in the Ten Commandments. Here we see, for instance, the priority of love in all relationships, the value of all human life, and the sanctity of marriage. These positions have been given to us by God Himself; therefore they are firm and cannot be compromised. Yet there is a danger in that for us—that we conduct our ministry by only addressing these earthly matters. There is always the temptation to become so

involved in social issues that we miss opportunities to share with the world eternal issues. Ultimately, these are what really matter.

Waiting for Christ's Return

As we continue our sojourn in the barren wilderness that is life in this fallen world, sometimes we can only sigh over the heartbreaking conditions we find at every hand. Christian love and charity demand that we aid our neighbor. Yet, while addressing the problems of today, we must never lose sight of what is coming soon.

For that reason, the Gospel of Christ is our chief treasure and the most important assistance we could ever offer anyone, regardless of their circumstances. For in our Lord Christ, we find the forgiveness of sins; and where there is forgiveness of sins, there is life everlasting. For those who have received the faith in Jesus, the Last Day is something to which we may look forward and count on all throughout our lives, especially during painful times. On that day when Christ returns, we will be raised from the dead, our bodies being refashioned after the perfection of Jesus Himself. We will live in the very presence of God—both in body and soul—on a new earth, one that no longer has the troubles and sorrows that we have been burdened with for so long. There, indeed, all the social and political ills of the world will find their perfect and lasting cure.

58

Study Guide

The Prophet Zechariah, Sistine Chapel, Erich Lessing/Art Resource, NY

LifeLight

LifeLight Expands

Available NOW!

The Bible: An Overview
Genesis, Pt. 1
Genesis, Pt. 2
Exodus, Pt. 1
Exodus, Pt. 2
Wilderness Wanderings
Joshua
Judges
Ruth/Esther
1 & 2 Samuel
Life of David
1 & 2 Kings

Ezra/Nehemiah
Job
Selected Psalms
Proverbs
Ecclesiastes/Song of Solomon
Isaiah, Pt. 1
Isaiah, Pt. 2
Daniel
Minor Prophets
Haggai/Zechariah/Malachi

Matthew, Pt. 1
Matthew, Pt. 2
Mark
Luke, Pt. 1
Luke, Pt. 2
John, Pt. 1
John, Pt. 2
Acts, Pt. 1
Acts, Pt. 2
Romans, Pt. 1
Romans, Pt. 2
1 Corinthians

2 Corinthians
Galatians/Philippians/Colossians
Ephesians/1 & 2 Thessalonians
Timothy/Titus/Philemon
Hebrews
James/Jude
1 & 2 Peter
1, 2, 3 John
Revelation

LifeLight Foundations

Baptism
Bible Feasts
Creation, New Creation

The Christian's Mission
Heaven & Hell
Law & Gospel

Ministry
Miracles
Prayer

Prophecy
Triune God
Worship

LifeLight Release Schedule

2013 RELEASES

LifeLight Foundations—Parables	October

2014 RELEASES

LifeLight—Nahum/Habakkuk/Zephaniah	January
LifeLight—1 & 2 Chronicles	April
LifeLight—Hosea/Joel/Amos	July
LifeLight Foundations—End Times	October

2015 RELEASES

LifeLight—Jeremiah/Lamentations	January
LifeLight—Ezekiel	April
LifeLight—Obadiah/Jonah/Micah	July

A New Start and a Coming Savior

Selected Passages

Distribute before session 1 for use in session 1.
Use enrichment magazine pp. 2–4.

Resources for Worship

Use these resources for your daily study at home and at the week's assembly.

Hymn

Speak, O Lord, Your servant listens,
Let Your Word to me come near;
Newborn life and spirit give me,
Let each promise still my fear.
Death's dread pow'r, its inward strife,
Wars against Your Word of life;
Fill me, Lord, with love's strong fervor
That I cling to You forever!

Oh, what blessing to be near You
And to listen to Your voice;
Let me ever love and hear You,
Let Your Word be now my choice!
Many hardened sinners, Lord,
Flee in terror at Your Word;
But to all who feel sin's burden
You give words of peace and pardon.

Lord, Your words are waters living
When my thirsting spirit pleads.
Lord, Your words are bread life-giving;
On Your words my spirit feeds.
Lord, Your words will be my light
Through death's cold and dreary night;
Yes, they are my sword prevailing
And my cup of joy unfailing!

As I pray, dear Jesus, hear me;
Let Your words in me take root.
May Your Spirit e'er be near me
That I bear abundant fruit.
May I daily sing Your praise,
From my heart glad anthems raise,
Till my highest praise is given
In the endless joy of heaven.
(*LSB* 589)

Prayer

Almighty God, Creator of heaven and earth, open our minds and hearts by the power of Your Holy Spirit, so that we may read Your Word and believe in what You have done for us in Jesus Christ, Your dear Son. When You brought Your chosen people back from their time of exile, You renewed Your precious promises to them and pointed their faith toward the coming Savior of the world. Through that same Word of truth, purify Your Church on earth, distinguish it from the evils of this world, and let Your mercy shine upon us in forgiveness until we come to that eternal life that You have prepared for us in Christ, for it is in His name we pray. Amen.

Digging Deep
My Personal Study for Week 1

Day 1 • Selected Passages

The Books of Haggai, Zechariah, and Malachi reflect upon the final phase of God's holy nation after the release of His people from exile and prior to the arrival of Jesus Christ. This week, before we delve into the books themselves, we will review what happened to Israel during and after the Babylonian exile.

1. Read Leviticus 26:27–45 and Deuteronomy 29:24–29. What, according to Moses, would eventually cause the children of Israel to go into exile?

2. Through His prophets, God told the Israelites that they would be in captivity.

a. Read Jeremiah 25:1–14. What was Jeremiah's prophecy regarding the length of the Babylonian exile?

b. How do you think this information would impact the faithful Israelites? See Leviticus 26:40–45.

3. a. Read Daniel 4:28–37. How does God's retribution against Babylon come in the days of King Nebuchadnezzar?

b. What similarities and differences are there between Nebuchadnezzar and the Persian King Cyrus? See 2 Chronicles 36:22–23.

4. Read Ezekiel 39:21–29. If you were one of Ezekiel's hearers still living in a land far from home, what would your response be to these words?

5. What is a remnant, as the term applies to Israel and the Church? See Genesis 45:4–7; Micah 2:12; Isaiah 10:20–22; and Romans 11:2–6.

Day 2 • Selected Passages

The passages today will examine the role of prophets.

6. Describe the roles that Samuel filled as a leader of Israel. How did he receive authority over the people? See 1 Samuel 2:18–19; 3:10–20; 7:8–12, 15–17; 8:4–7; 9:15–19; and 13:9–13.

7. a. Read Deuteronomy 18:18–22. By what criteria would the people evaluate the prophets who claim to be sent from God?

b. How was the prophecy in verse 18 ultimately fulfilled?

8. a. Read Ezekiel 33:7–9. Ezekiel was a prophet during the Babylonian captivity. Why would he not be held accountable when people rejected the Lord's Word and forfeited salvation?

b. Now consider our Christian pastors of today according to this same standard. For what reasons should pastors be blamed if members under their care turn away from the faith? What commendation is appropriate for a pastor when a congregation succeeds? See also Luke 17:10.

9. Read Hebrews 1:1–4. Are Christians to expect new prophecies or revelations sent by God? Why or why not?

New Temple, New Challenges

Haggai 1

Distribute before session 2 for use in session 2.
Use enrichment magazine pp. 5–7.

Resources for Worship

Use these resources for your daily study at home and at the week's assembly.

Hymn

If thou but trust in God to guide thee
  And hope in Him through all thy ways,
He'll give thee strength, whate'er betide thee,
  And bear thee through the evil days.
Who trusts in God's unchanging love
Builds on the rock that naught can move.

God knows full well when times of gladness
  Shall be the needful thing for thee.
When He has tried thy soul with sadness
  And from all guile has found thee free,
He comes to thee all unaware
And makes thee own His loving care.

Nor think amid the fiery trial
  That God hath cast thee off unheard,
That he whose hopes meet no denial
  Must surely be of God preferred.
Time passes and much change doth bring
And sets a bound to ev'rything.

Sing, pray, and keep His ways unswerving,
  Perform thy duties faithfully,
And trust His Word; though undeserving,
  Thou yet shalt find it true for thee.
God never yet forsook in need
The soul that trusted Him indeed.
(*LSB* 750:1, 4, 5, 7)

Prayer

Almighty God, who is greater than the highest heavens yet is still pleased to dwell with us on earth, forgive us when we take Your abundant mercy for granted. Impress upon us a renewed sense of Your grace to us in Christ, our Savior, so that we may always come before You with grateful hearts and consecrated minds. Let nothing distract us from true devotion to You, and lead us to receive all Your blessings with a proper perspective, knowing that our true home is being prepared for us with You in heaven. Amen.

Digging Deep
My Personal Study for Week 2

Day 1 • Read Haggai 1:1–2

1. What were some events that contributed to a delay in rebuilding the Jerusalem temple? Refer to Ezra 4:1–5 and 5:1–12.

2. Read Ezra 1:1–8; 3:1–7; Deuteronomy 30:1–10; and Isaiah 44:21–45:7. In what ways did God bring about the fulfillment of His promise concerning the temple?

3. Who were the two specific men singled out in Haggai's prophetic message at the beginning of chapter 1? Why was the complaint directed to them first?

4. In what ways does procrastination signal a lack of faith in one's personal life? in the life of a church?

5. **Challenge question.** Is it appropriate for Christian congregations to consider whether it is God's will that they build a worship or other ministry space? Why or why not?

Day 2 • Read Haggai 1:3–6

6. Based on their actions in Haggai 1:3–6, the people of Jerusalem held what priorities as the highest?

7. Read 2 Samuel 7:1–3. What was King David's desire? Why do you think the prophet Nathan at first allowed him to proceed with his plan?

8. Read 2 Samuel 7:4–17. What are the two meanings of the word "house" in this passage? What was God's promise intended for David and those after him?

9. What are some good and proper ways in which we can show thankfulness to God? See 2 Samuel 7:18–29 and Matthew 26:6–13.

10. Suppose a trusted friend of yours wants to give something to your church worth more than half of its yearly budget, whether as a bequest written in a will or as an outright gift. If you were to counsel this benefactor, what actions and attitudes would you encourage and discourage in this act of generosity? Discuss Bible passages that may serve as your guide.

Day 3 • Read Haggai 1:7–11

11. What concrete directions did God give to the people in order to build His temple?

The Lord Whom You Seek

Haggai 2

Distribute before session 3 for use in session 3.
Use enrichment magazine pp. 8–9.

Resources for Worship

Use these resources for your daily study at home and at the week's assembly.

Hymn

Christ is made the sure foundation,
  Christ, our head and cornerstone,
Chosen of the Lord and precious,
  Binding all the Church in one;
Holy Zion's help forever
  And our confidence alone.

To this temple, where we call You,
  Come, O Lord of hosts, and stay;
Come with all Your loving-kindness,
  Hear Your people as they pray;
And Your fullest benediction
  Shed within these walls today.

Grant, we pray, to all Your faithful
  All the gifts they ask to gain;
What they gain from You, forever
  With the blessèd to retain;
And hereafter in Your glory
  Evermore with You to reign.
(*LSB* 909:1–3)

Prayer

O Lord God of hosts, who comes to shake the heavens and the earth, and who has promised to fill Your house with glory, we confess that we have defiled the honor of Your Word with unholy thoughts, words, and deeds. We have selfishly kept to ourselves the gifts that truly belong to You. Do not remove Your Spirit from our midst, but strengthen and purify us so that we may serve You with true and confident faith. Form us in Your image, for we are Your signet ring that carries out Your will on earth, and through Your Church obtain for Yourself a kingdom in the name of Jesus Christ, our Lord. Amen.

Digging Deep
My Personal Study for Week 3

Day 1 • Read Haggai 2:1–5

1. Read Ezra 3:8–13. Ezra was a contemporary of Haggai. What two distinct emotional responses accompanied the ceremony at the laying of the new temple's foundation?

2. Why was it discouraging for the people to be building a much smaller and simpler house of worship, as compared to what they remembered of Solomon's temple?

3. If you were to consider, on a scale of 1 to 10, with the temple building by itself on one end and the Lord's promise to dwell by grace on the other, where would you place the following:

a. The object of King Solomon's faith (See 1 Kings 8:27–30.)

b. The faith of the people rebuilding the temple (See Haggai 2:3.)

Assuming there is a difference, why do you think that the object of faith had changed?

4. Haggai 2:5 includes the words "My Spirit remains in your midst."

a. Compare this statement with other references to the Holy Spirit. What did the Holy Spirit do for people in the Old Testament? See Genesis 1:2; Psalm 51:11; and Joel 2:28–29.

b. Now consider Ezekiel 36:25–27. What was yet to come for the Spirit to do in the New Testament era?

5. Haggai was given three divine commands for the people as they faced a very difficult undertaking: Be strong! Work! Fear not! Share with one another what is comforting about these words for you in your Christian life of faith and actions.

Day 2 • Read Haggai 2:6–9

6. According to Haggai 2:7–9, what will happen when the Lord shakes the nations of the earth?

7. At the time of Haggai, the temple was still restricted to Israelites; Gentiles were not allowed in its holy courts. How would the Gentiles be involved in the future glory of God's house? (See Ephesians 2:11–16.)

8. Read Hebrews 12:25–29.

a. What is the reason for God to be shaking the present creation? (Consider also 2 Thessalonians 1:7–9.)

b. What does this shaking in Hebrews 12:28 mean for believers?

c. If we are guaranteed to receive God's gift of a kingdom that cannot be shaken, then why should we still be concerned about "acceptable worship, with reverence and awe" (Hebrews 12:28)?

Visions of Jerusalem
Zechariah 1–4

Distribute before session 4 for use in session 4.
Use enrichment magazine pp. 10–12.

Resources for Worship

Use these resources for your daily study at home and at the week's assembly.

Hymn

The day is surely drawing near
 When Jesus, God's anointed,
In all His power shall appear
 As judge whom God appointed.
Then fright shall banish idle mirth,
And flames on flames shall ravage earth
 As Scripture long has warned us.

The final trumpet then shall sound
 And all the earth be shaken,
And all who rest beneath the ground
 Shall from their sleep awaken.
But all who live will in that hour,
By God's almighty, boundless pow'r,
 Be changed at His commanding.

The books are opened then to all,
 A record truly telling
What each has done, both great and small,
 When he on earth was dwelling,
And ev'ry heart be clearly seen,
And all be known as they have been
 In thoughts and words and actions.

Then woe to those who scorned the Lord
 And sought but carnal pleasures,
Who here despised His precious Word
 And loved their earthly treasures!
With shame and trembling they will stand
And at the judge's stern command
 To Satan be delivered.

My Savior paid the debt I owe
 And for my sin was smitten;
Within the Book of Life I know
 My name has now been written.
I will not doubt, for I am free,
And Satan cannot threaten me;
 There is no condemnation!

May Christ our intercessor be
 And through His blood and merit
Read from His book that we are free
 With all who life inherit.
Then we shall see Him face to face,
With all His saints in that blest place
 Which He has purchased for us.

O Jesus Christ, do not delay,
 But hasten our salvation;
We often tremble on our way
 In fear and tribulation.
O hear and grant our fervent plea:
Come, mighty judge, and set us free
 From death and ev'ry evil.
(*LSB* 508)

Prayer

Protect us, merciful Father, from everything that threatens our faith in You. Without Your angels guarding over us, our souls will never find rest on earth, for Satan and his forces constantly mount their attacks. But since You have gained the victory over our enemies through the blood of Jesus Christ, Your Son, we pray that our hearts may be fixed on Him as our Savior, the Branch, the One who purifies us in Baptism and plants us by pure grace into the fellowship of Your Holy Church forever. Grant that Your kingdom may come among us, not by might, nor by power, but by Your Holy Spirit, for the sake of Christ, our Lord, and all that He has done for us. Amen.

Digging Deep
My Personal Study for Week 4

Day 1 • Read Zechariah 1:1–6

1. According to Zechariah's inspired introductory words, what was the chief point that the exile was meant to drive home to the new generation?

2. Read and take note of the word *return* in Deuteronomy 4:27–31; Psalm 90:13; and Joel 2:12–14. Normally, "return" means "come back" or "give back." What does it mean in the spiritual sense?

3. What is God remembering in these passages?

Genesis 8:1

Exodus 2:24

Psalm 115:12

Jeremiah 14:10

Jeremiah 31:34

Zechariah's name means "the LORD remembers." What do you think the significance would be of this prophet having that name?

4. We can note that, as well as being a prophet, Zechariah was also a priest (Ezra 8:15–16). Skim 1 Chronicles 6:1–15 and Ezra 2:59–63. Why did Old Testament priests pay special attention to their genealogy? What would happen if they could not provide proof of their heritage?

5. Read Isaiah 40:6–8 and 2 Timothy 4:1–8. What responsibility does the finite preacher have regarding the eternal Word of God?

Day 2 • Read Zechariah 1:7–21

6. What does Zechariah see in his first night vision (vv. 7–17), and what message does he receive about the exile?

7. Verse 11 reveals that the Angel of the Lord is central to Zechariah's vision.

a. Read the following appearances of the Angel of the Lord. What evidence do you see in these passages that the Angel of the Lord has majesty equal to that of the Lord?

Genesis 22:9–18

Exodus 3:1–6

Numbers 22:22–35

Judges 13:1–5, 15–24

b. Note that in Zechariah 1:12, the Angel of the Lord interceded on behalf of the exiles. Read Romans 8:31–34 and Hebrews 7:22–28. What is Jesus doing when we pray?

The Coming of the Branch

Zechariah 5–8

Distribute before session 5 for use in session 5.
Use enrichment magazine pp. 13–15.

Resources for Worship

Use these resources for your daily study at home and at the week's assembly.

Hymn

The Church's one foundation
Is Jesus Christ, her Lord;
She is His new creation
By water and the Word.
From heav'n He came and sought her
To be His holy bride;
With His own blood He bought her,
And for her life He died.

Elect from ev'ry nation,
Yet one o'er all the earth;
Her charter of salvation:
One Lord, one faith, one birth.
One holy name she blesses,
Partakes one holy food,
And to one hope she presses
With ev'ry grace endued.

Though with a scornful wonder
The world sees her oppressed,
By schisms rent asunder,
By heresies distressed,
Yet saints their watch are keeping;
Their cry goes up, "How long?"
And soon the night of weeping
Shall be the morn of song.

Through toil and tribulation
And tumult of her war
She waits the consummation
Of peace forevermore
Till with the vision glorious
Her longing eyes are blest,
And the great Church victorious
Shall be the Church at rest.

Yet she on earth has union
With God, the Three in One,
And mystic sweet communion
With those whose rest is won.
O blessèd heav'nly chorus!
Lord, save us by Your grace
That we, like saints before us,
May see You face to face.
(*LSB* 644)

Prayer

Lord God, heavenly Father, in these latter days, we beseech You to build Your Church and grant us strength to face the challenges of our society around us. Lead us to be merciful, just as Your Son Jesus, during the ministry of His flesh, was merciful to all who sought Him in faith. Open our ears to hear Your precious Word that sustains Your people from day to day. And when the Final Day comes, the Day when our Savior will return in glory, graciously receive us into the kingdom of glory that He has prepared for us through His sacrificial blood. In His name we pray, Amen.

Digging Deep
My Personal Study for Week 5

Day 1 • Read Zechariah 5

1. What is symbolized by the flying scroll in Zechariah's vision?

2. **Challenge question.** It is interesting to note that the measurements of the flying scroll are the same as the measurements listed for the Holy Place in the tabernacle and Solomon's temple. (Compare 1 Kings 6:3.) What do you think this suggests about the curse that God is here pronouncing?

3. The woman in a basket (Zechariah 5:5–8) is identified with "Wickedness." What would be the ultimate form of wickedness? Consider Isaiah 42:8 and Matthew 4:10.

4. Read Genesis 11:1–9 and Daniel 1:2. Where was the land of Shinar, mentioned in Zechariah 5:11, and for what was it notorious?

5. **Challenge question.** What do you think it means that, in the vision in Zechariah 5:11, a house was built for the woman in Shinar?

Day 2 • Read Zechariah 6

6. How are chariots used to reveal God's power in 2 Kings 2:10–12 and 6:15–18?

7. a. What did the kingdoms in the "north country" (Assyria and Babylon) do to Israel and Judah? Why? See 2 Kings 17:1–6 and 2 Chronicles 36:17–21.

b. Read Jeremiah 1:13–19. What do you think it means that God's Spirit has been set at rest in the "north country" (Zechariah 6:8)?

8. Read Exodus 29:6 and 39:30–31.

a. What crown did the high priest normally wear?

b. What did the crown in Zechariah 6:9–14 foretell about the twofold ministry of the promised Christ?

The Shepherd Saves the Sheep
Zechariah 9–11

Distribute before session 6 for use in session 6.
Use enrichment magazine pp. 16–18.

Resources for Worship

Use these resources for your daily study at home and at the week's assembly.

Hymn

Rejoice, O pilgrim throng!
    Rejoice, give thanks, and sing;
Your festal banner wave on high,
    The cross of Christ your king.
Rejoice! Rejoice! Rejoice, give thanks, and sing!

With voice as full and strong
    As ocean's surging praise,
Send forth the sturdy hymns of old,
    The psalms of ancient days.
Rejoice! Rejoice! Rejoice, give thanks, and sing!

With all the angel choirs,
    With all the saints on earth
Pour out the strains of joy and bliss,
    True rapture, noblest mirth.
Rejoice! Rejoice! Rejoice, give thanks, and sing!

Yet on and onward still,
    With hymn and chant and song,
Through gate and porch and columned aisle
    The hallowed pathways throng.
Rejoice! Rejoice! Rejoice, give thanks, and sing!

At last the march shall end;
    The wearied ones shall rest;
The pilgrims find their home at last,
    Jerusalem the blest.
Rejoice! Rejoice! Rejoice, give thanks, and sing!
(*LSB* 813:1–4, 6)

Prayer

We rejoice, O Lord Jesus, our King, in Your lowly coming among us, humbly wrapped first in flesh and blood and now given to us in Word, water, bread, and wine. We admit, as a struggling, tempted, stubborn, and battered daughter of Zion, that we have done what is worthy of nothing but punishment now and forever. But we thank You for Your full and ultimate salvation, which You won for us on the cross and proclaimed through the empty tomb and for Your words of peace. Forgive us our sins and grant us a new heart to shout and sing aloud for joy so that all the world may know of the eternal life that You won for our sake and for the rescue of all people. Grant this for the sake of Your holy name. Amen.

Digging Deep
My Personal Study for Week 6

Day 1 • Read Zechariah 9:1–8

1. What was the oracle or burden (v. 1) of prophecy against prominent cities and countries just outside Israel's borders?

2. How did Israel's relationship with Tyre develop? See 2 Samuel 5:11–12; 1 Kings 5:1–12; and 9:10–14.

3. Why did God delay the final punishment of the enemies of His people? See Genesis 15:13–16 and 2 Peter 3:9.

4. a. Read Joshua 15:63. Who were the Jebusites? Where did they live?

b. Read 2 Samuel 5:6–10 and 1 Kings 9:20–21. What happened to the Jebusites after David conquered them?

5. Throughout the Old Testament, the term "remnant" is applied to God's people. What does the use of this term for the people of the destroyed nations reveal about God's plan for them (Zechariah 9:7)? How would they become a remnant? See Matthew 8:5–13.

Day 2 • Read Zechariah 9:9–13

6. What is the reason for rejoicing and celebration?

7. What two processions of Jesus are foretold by Zechariah here? See Matthew 21:1–11 and 1 Thessalonians 4:16–17.

8. Read Isaiah 52:1–3; 62:8–12; and Jeremiah 6:22–26. When these prophets use the name "daughter of Zion," what are they usually describing about the spiritual condition of Jerusalem and its people?

9. Refer to your answer to Question 8. When Zechariah uses the name "daughter of Zion," what is he remembering about Israel's past? What is he assuring God's people about their future?

10. Read Zechariah 9:11 and Hebrews 9:18–26. How does Christ's blood of the covenant set believers free?

Day 3 • Read Zechariah 9:14–17

11. How will the Lord's people gain victory over their enemies?

All Nations Shall Worship Him

Zechariah 12–14

Distribute before session 7 for use in session 7.
Use enrichment magazine pp. 22–26.

Resources for Worship

Use these resources for your daily study at home and at the week's assembly.

Hymn

I love Your kingdom, Lord,
The place of Your abode,
The Church our blest Redeemer saved
With His own precious blood.

Beyond my highest joy
I prize its heav'nly ways,
Its sweet communion, solemn vows,
Its hymns of love and praise.

I love Your Church, O God,
Your saints in ev'ry land,
Dear as the apple of Your eye
And graven on Your hand.

Sure as Your truth shall last,
To Zion shall be giv'n
The brightest glories earth can yield
And brighter bliss of heav'n.
(*LSB* 651:1–3, 5)

Prayer

O Christ, our Good Shepherd, on the cross You were struck with suffering and death for the deliverance of Your precious sheep. You were pierced through with deadly wounds so that we might be healed from our sins. We pray that, as You promised salvation to Your people through the mouth of Zechariah long ago, You would in our day encourage us with that same Gospel Word of forgiveness and eternal life, until the final Day when You return in glory and we are fully ransomed from the tribulations of this world. Hear us for the sake of Your holy name. Amen.

Digging Deep
My Personal Study for Week 7

Day 1 • Read Zechariah 12:1–9

1. In this passage, the expression "on that day" ties this prophecy to the end times. What will be the fate of the enemy nations who attack Jerusalem, which is a symbol of the Church?

2. Read verses 1 and 9. What right does God claim for Himself because He is the Creator of the universe? Does this disturb you or fill you with hope? Explain.

3. Read verse 2; Isaiah 63:1–6; and Jeremiah 25:15–29.

a. What does the cup of wine represent?

b. What does it mean when God chooses His people to be the wine that makes other nations stagger with drunkenness?

4. What are the images used by Zechariah to depict God's complete victory in the battle against His enemies?

5. **Challenge question.** Although Christ has built His Church and "the gates of hell shall not prevail against it" (Matthew 16:18), the Church must still engage in spiritual conflict. What do you think we should remember as we find ourselves in this struggle?

Day 2 • Read Zechariah 12:10–14

6. How is it possible for God to be pierced, as Zechariah predicts (v. 10)? See John 19:34–37 and Acts 3:13–15.

7. What was so significant about Hadad-rimmon in Megiddo (12:11) that Zechariah refers to it when he speaks of the mourning in Jerusalem? See 2 Kings 23:29–30 and 2 Chronicles 35:20–25.

8. Read Luke 23:27–31. Why does Jesus tell the women not to weep for Him?

9. The death of Jesus, as well as His being pierced as Zechariah prophesied, is commemorated on Good Friday. What is the most memorable part of a Good Friday service for you? Why does that stick out in your mind?

Day 3 • Read Zechariah 13:1–6

10. Verse 1 speaks of a fountain to cleanse believers from sin. How does this cleaning take place (1 John 1:7)?

11. Read Numbers 8:5–22, taking special note of verse 7. How would the cleansing of the Levites in the Old Testament foreshadow that of the royal priesthood of believers in the era of the New Testament? See also Acts 22:16 and Romans 6:3–4.

Malachi, My Messenger

Malachi 1–2

Distribute before session 8 for use in session 8.
Use enrichment magazine pp. 27–29.

Resources for Worship

Use these resources for your daily study at home and at the week's assembly.

Hymn

We give Thee but Thine own,
Whate'er the gift may be;
All that we have is Thine alone,
A trust, O Lord, from Thee.

May we Thy bounties thus
As stewards true receive
And gladly, as Thou blessest us,
To Thee our firstfruits give!

The captive to release,
To God the lost to bring,
To teach the way of life and peace,
It is a Christ-like thing.

And we believe Thy Word,
Though dim our faith may be:
Whate'er for Thine we do, O Lord,
We do it unto Thee.
(*LSB* 781:1–2, 5–6)

Prayer

Heavenly Father, guard our lips with Your saving knowledge. You have abundantly showered us with blessings. You have honored Your promises and remained faithful to us, even though we have disobeyed You in thought, word, and deed. Before our sins harden our hearts and seriously damage our relationship with You, grant us repentance, forgiveness, and purification by Your Word. Bind us to You in the marriage covenant of faith, so that we may look forward with expectant joy as we await the second coming of our Messiah, Jesus, in whose name we pray. Amen.

Digging Deep
My Personal Study for Week 8

Day 1 • Read Malachi 1:1–5

1. In this section of Malachi, reference is made to Esau and his brother, Jacob. Recall that in Genesis, God blessed Abraham and promised him and his descendants an inheritance. This promise was passed on to his son Isaac, who had two sons, Esau and Jacob. The blessing was passed on to Jacob, even though he was the younger of the two. Esau's descendants became the Edomites. What happened centuries later when Jacob's descendants (Israel) journeyed from Egypt to the Promised Land (Numbers 20:14–21)?

2. How did God show His love to Jacob's descendants, Israel? See Hosea 11:1.

3. It can be disturbing for us to read the statement from God in Malachi 1:3, "but Esau I have hated." How can this expression of God's "hatred" be best understood? Consider Exodus 33:19; Romans 9:9–16; and 1 Timothy 2:4.

4. How were the Edomites in Malachi's prophecy (1:4) revealing a Babellike attitude (Genesis 11:1–9)?

5. *For personal reflection. Sharing optional.* Think about someone in your life who claimed that, for him or her, God has withheld His love. How did you respond? What assurance did or would you give to someone like that?

Day 2 • Read Malachi 1:6–10

6. a. What was God's standard for the animals offered as sacrifices (Leviticus 22:20–22)?

b. What ceremonial offenses were the priests committing that revealed their contempt for God's name (Malachi 1:7–8)?

7. How did the Judean worship practice get restarted after the Babylonian exile? See Ezra 7:11–25 and Nehemiah 10:32–39.

8. Even though the priests were violating God's prescriptions for the sacrifices, they assumed their polluted sacrifices would be acceptable through frequent repetition. Consider Isaiah 29:13–21 and Mark 7:6–13. What damage can man-made traditions do to the commandments of God?

9. **Challenge question.** How can traditions and ceremonies be used properly so that they strengthen faith, instead of destroying it?

10. Read 1 Chronicles 21:14–27. Why did David insist on paying for the land upon which he was to sacrifice to the Lord? What is Malachi's point of using the best for sacrifice, rather than the leftovers?

The Coming Messenger

Malachi 3–4

Distribute before session 9 for use in session 9.
Use enrichment magazine pp. 30–32.

Resources for Worship

Use these resources for your daily study at home and at the week's assembly.

Hymn

Jesus, lead Thou on
Till our rest is won;
  And although the way be cheerless,
  We will follow calm and fearless.
Guide us by Thy hand
To our fatherland.

If the way be drear,
If the foe be near,
  Let not faithless fears o'ertake us;
  Let not faith and hope forsake us;
For through many a woe
To our home we go.

When we seek relief
From a long-felt grief,
  When temptations come alluring,
  Make us patient and enduring.
Show us that bright shore
Where we weep no more.

Jesus, lead Thou on
Till our rest is won.
  Heav'nly leader, still direct us,
  Still support, console, protect us,
Till we safely stand
In our fatherland.
(*LSB* 718)

Prayer

Almighty and eternal God and Father, You have promised everlasting life to us in Jesus Christ, our Savior. You have sent us prophets and apostles and messengers to proclaim Your Word to us and turn our hearts to You in repentance. Forgive us for when we have not shown a strong faith in You through our gifts, tithes, and hearts. Open Your book of remembrance and record our names for now and for eternity, especially since we have not done anything to deserve Your favor, but Jesus has granted us His heavenly inheritance. Heal us under Your wings and let the sun of Your grace shine with Your abundant pardon, so that we may not be put to shame but rather leap with joy for all that You have done for us. In the name of Jesus we pray. Amen.

Digging Deep
My Personal Study for Week 9

Day 1 • Read Malachi 3:1–5

Beginning in chapter 3, Malachi departs from the topic of priestly corruption to highlight the coming of the promised Messiah, our Lord Jesus.

1. What role does Scripture assign to John the Baptist? See Isaiah 40:3–5; Matthew 3:1–6; Luke 1:76–80; John 1:19–34; and 3:27–30.

2. What is the Lord going to do when He suddenly appears at His temple, according to Malachi's prophecy (3:1)? See also John 2:19–22.

3. Malachi 1–2 talks of the corruption of the priesthood. Now, in Malachi 3:3–4, we hear of its purification.

a. What purification did the sons of Levi need (Malachi 1:6–8; 2:7–9)?

b. What is this purified priesthood today (1 Peter 2:4–9)?

4. **Challenge question.** Why do you suppose that, even with a messenger preparing the way before Him, the Lord's appearance still happened "suddenly"?

Day 2 • Read Malachi 3:6–11

5. Read Numbers 18:21–29 and Nehemiah 12:44–47; 13:10–12. What were the requirements for the tithes in the time of the Old Testament? What practical benefits did this practice give to the Levites? to the laypeople?

6. What does Malachi mean when he says that God's people rob Him (3:8–10)?

7. Why does God ask to be tested in verse 10? See Psalm 34:8.

8. a. The tithe system was part of the Law given through Moses. Are Christians obligated to tithe? Consider Matthew 5:17 and Galatians 3:1–14, 24–25.

b. What do the following texts reveal about Christian giving?

1 Corinthians 16:1–2

2 Corinthians 8:1–8

9. **Challenge question.** Do you think it is right for a Christian to give an offering or tithe in the expectation of receiving a blessing from God in exchange? Why or why not?

Day 3 • Read Malachi 3:12–15

10. Read verse 12 and Deuteronomy 28:1–14. What blessings would the nations observe in Israel if her people remained faithful?

11. Read Malachi 3:14–15, and skim Psalm 73 and Jeremiah 12. What is the best comfort for those who are discouraged because the wicked seem always to prosper?

12. Malachi 3:13–15 speaks of where God's people accuse Him of unfairness. Now read Luke 15:11–32. What was the objection of the older brother? How did he also despise the father's love?

13. Read Matthew 20:1–16. In what ways are believers tempted to begrudge God's generosity? How can you fight this temptation?

Day 4 • Read Malachi 3:16–18

14. What was the Lord's promise to those who had remained faithful to Him (v. 16)?

15. Read 2 Corinthians 1:3–7. What does God want His children to speak to one another (Malachi 3:16)?

16. How do you think tragedy or turmoil could bring a congregation closer together? What do you think would need to be done to ensure that suffering leads to comfort and not destruction?

17. **Challenge question.** A book of remembrance was used by a king to establish a public record that could not be reversed. What do you think God's "book of remembrance" reveals about Him and His relationship with His people in these readings?

Psalm 139:14–16

Daniel 12:1

Philippians 4:3

Revelation 20:11–15

18. a. How does Malachi describe the "distinction between the righteous and the wicked" (v. 18)?

b. How is this righteousness attained (Romans 3:21–26)?

Day 5 • Read Malachi 4

19. Read verses 1–3 and Isaiah 26:10–15. What hope is there for turmoil-stricken Christians who notice that wicked people exist among them, even within their church?

20. **Challenge question.** Read Malachi 4:4–5 and Hebrews 3:1–6. What did Moses' work point to?

21. Read Malachi 4:5 and Matthew 11:7–15. When was "Elijah" sent before the Day of the Lord?

22. Read Malachi 4:5–6 and Luke 3:1–17. How was John the Baptist turning "the hearts of fathers to their children and . . . children to their fathers" (v. 6)? What similarities to Malachi do you see in John's preaching?

Day 3 • Read Malachi 1:11–14

11. What does God desire from all the Gentile nations (v. 11)?

12. How were the priests' sins affecting the Lord's ultimate plan of salvation?

13. Read Luke 21:1–4. Even though the widow gave the smallest offering, why was Jesus commending her over the rich people who gave abundantly?

14. **Challenge question.** Reread verse 14. How may vows and pledges be used rightly in the church? What abuses should be avoided?

Day 4 • Read Malachi 2:1–9

15. What instruction was the Lord expecting the priests to give to the people (vv. 6–7)? Recall Nehemiah 8:8.

16. Read Malachi 2:2 and Numbers 6:22–27 (note that Aaron and his sons were called to be priests for the people). How did God choose to distribute His blessing to the Church, then and now?

17. Read Malachi 2:2, 8. If a priest despised the name of the Lord with false teaching or sinful life, then what happened to the blessing that he pronounced in the name of the Lord? Consider also Deuteronomy 18:20–22 and James 3:1.

18. **Challenge question.** Read Malachi 2:8–9 and James 2:1–13. In what way does the sin of showing partiality do damage to the Gospel and the Church?

Day 5 • Read Malachi 2:10–17

19. Malachi turns from his rebuke of the priesthood to the sins of the people. What sins did he decry (vv. 11, 15–16)?

20. Why were these sins so damaging? See Deuteronomy 7:3–4 and 2 Corinthians 6:14–18.

21. Read Deuteronomy 24:1–4 and Matthew 19:1–9. Within what parameters was divorce permitted in the Law of Moses? What does Jesus explain about this Old Testament civil law?

22. **Challenge question.** Read Ephesians 5:25–32. Notice that there is a parallel between the union of a husband and wife and that of Christ and His Church. Suppose a believing husband were to despise his wife and divorce her in order to marry an unbelieving woman. What witness would he then have given about Christ?

12. Read Zechariah 13:3 and Matthew 10:34–39. In what situations does Jesus command us actually to be "enemies" with the people of our own family?

13. **Challenge question.** Zechariah 13:3 refers to the lies of false prophets. What tricks do the false prophets of our day use to try to deceive people? What makes it so easy for many to believe them?

Day 4 • Read Zechariah 13:7–9

14. a. Verse 7 contains a prophecy involving the striking of a shepherd. How is this prophecy fulfilled? See John 10:14 and Mark 14:43–52.

b. How are the scattered sheep gathered together again? See Matthew 26:31 and 28:10–16.

15. How does this result in the salvation of a faithful remnant, according to Zechariah 13:8–9?

16. For what purpose does God allow His redeemed children to undergo sufferings in this world (Zechariah 13:9)? See also Romans 5:3–5 and 8:18–39.

17. Why did God reduce Israel down to a remnant (Zechariah 13:8–9)? How did this accomplish His greater purpose of salvation for all nations? See also 1 Kings 19:9–18 and Romans 11:1–12.

Day 5 • Read Zechariah 14

18. Verses 1–2 contain a prophecy about how the world will treat believers. What should believers know to expect? Also see Matthew 24:3–9 and John 16:33.

19. How is the Lord depicted saving His people (Zechariah 14:3–16)?

20. Read Zechariah 14:8; Ezekiel 47:1–12; and Revelation 22:1–5.

a. What is the source for the flowing fresh water in each of the three visions?

b. What is the fulfillment of these prophecies (John 4:9–14; 7:37–39)?

c. What do you think is significant about the water flowing in two directions (Zechariah 14:9; Revelation 7:9–10)?

21. Read Zechariah 14:16 and Leviticus 23:33–43. How was the Feast of Booths celebrated? What did it commemorate?

22. **Challenge question.** Read Nehemiah 8:13–18. This celebration of the Feast of Booths was held after Zechariah's prophecy was recorded. As well as being a remembrance of God's mercies in the past, what did this festival now anticipate for Israel's future?

12. What did blowing the trumpet (v. 14) signify for the armies of Israel? See Leviticus 23:23–27; Joshua 6:1–17; and Judges 7:19–23.

13. Read 1 Corinthians 15:51–57. What will *this* trumpet blast signify?

14. **Challenge question.** How does Zechariah's metaphor of God's people being like crown jewels (9:16) help us to understand the parable of the treasure in the field and the pearl of great value (Matthew 13:44–46)?

15. While the excessive consumption of wine is prohibited in Scripture, the imagery of drunkenness is used in the Bible to depict various things. What are the images of drunkenness depicted in each of these passages?

Psalm 78:65–66

Isaiah 51:17–23

Zechariah 9:15

Day 4 • Read Zechariah 10

16. Read verse 2 and Psalm 115. Even though it was clearly apparent that man-made gods were worthless, why did people nevertheless seek their help?

17. Read Zechariah 10:1 and Joel 2:21–27. What is given when God allows a full cycle of rain to fall on the land? What is removed?

18. Read Zechariah 10:1; John 16:22–24; and Romans 8:34. What new access did Jesus give to His disciples that they had not yet utilized?

19. Read Zechariah 10:2–3; Ezekiel 34:7–16; John 10:14–18, 27–28; and 1 Peter 5:1–3. How does God seek out and gather together His scattered sheep?

20. **Challenge question.** Which of the two would you consider to be the greater sign of God's blessing for a believer: a life of ease and plenty or a painful existence of suffering and anxiety? Or perhaps neither? Is it always wrong to expect good things from God in this life? Explain your answer.

Day 5 • Read Zechariah 11

21. Previously, the Lord seems to have simply spoken His prophecies to Zechariah or given them to him in the form of visions. In what new way is the Lord now delivering His Word of prophecy to Zechariah (v. 4)?

22. Read Zechariah 11:5–6 and Isaiah 65:11–15. What does Isaiah predict will happen to the Israelites who forsake the Lord, namely, Jesus the Messiah?

23. Read Zechariah 11:12; Exodus 21:32; and Matthew 26:15. Thirty pieces of silver was the replacement value for what? When that amount was paid for Judas's betrayal of Jesus, what did it reveal about how the Jewish leaders regarded Christ?

24. The shepherding of the flock doomed to be slaughtered and the breaking of the two staffs, Favor and Union, can be described as an "action prophecy." It was a prophecy that God had Zechariah proclaim through a demonstration rather than through preaching.

a. What did the breaking of the staff called "Favor" signify (Zechariah 11:7, 10–11)?

b. What did the breaking of the staff called "Union" signify (v. 14)?

c. Who, therefore, are the sheep doomed for slaughter?

Day 3 • Read Zechariah 7

9. A delegation from Bethel was sent to ask about a long-standing practice.

a. In verses 2–6, with what manner of worship were the messengers from Bethel trying to entreat the favor of the Lord?

b. What happened "in the fifth month" (2 Kings 25:8–9)?

c. What was wrong with their practice (Zechariah 7:4–6)?

d. What did Zechariah say was the truly genuine worship of God (7:9–10)?

e. How did the people respond (7:11)?

10. Read Romans 14. Today, we may not have the temptation to look down upon a fellow Christian because of what he eats or doesn't eat, but we are tempted by other forms of piety. What are some, and how could these possibly lead to disagreement with others? How could mutual Christian love be used to resolve the conflict?

11. Read 1 Kings 12:26–33. What notorious event took place in Bethel? Why didn't Jeroboam want any of his subjects to worship at the true temple in Jerusalem?

12. Read Zechariah 7:9–10 and 1 John 4:19–21. Because we do not have to do good things for our neighbor as a requirement for our salvation, how do acts of mercy relate to our faith?

Day 4 • Read Zechariah 8:1–13

13. What phrase is repeated over and over in chapter 8? What does this demonstrate about Zechariah's message?

14. What are the "hosts" in these passages?

Genesis 2:1

1 Kings 22:19

Isaiah 6:1–3

Psalm 24:10

Malachi 1:14

15. Compare Zechariah 8:1–13 with Exodus 20:1–17, especially verse 5. What actions are connected to God's jealousy in each?

16. What is meant by the "sowing of peace" (Zechariah 8:12–13)?

17. See Luke 2:14; 19:38; and Ephesians 2:13–18. How does Jesus bring peace on earth?

Day 5 • Read Zechariah 8:14–23

18. According to Zechariah's prophecy, how do people of outside nations gain the Lord's favor?

19. Read Ezekiel 33:10–11 and Romans 2:1–8. What is God's true desire for all people? What must He do if someone stubbornly rejects Him?

20. What are the "judgments that are true and make for peace" (Zechariah 8:16–17)? How do they relate to Jesus' exhortation in Luke 6:31?

21. Reread Zechariah 7:3 and 8:18–19. Here God, through the prophet Zechariah, addresses the practice of mournful fasts engaged in by the returned exiles.

a. What were the events of the Babylonian invasion that were remembered by annual fasts throughout the year? See 2 Kings 25:1–12, 25–26.

b. What does God provide for His broken, repentant people? See Zechariah 8:19 and Isaiah 61:1–3.

c. Consider your answers to (a) and (b) above. Whom does the Angel of the Lord appear to be?

8. **Challenge question.** God used other nations, such as Babylon, to chastise and scatter His people of Judah as He had previously threatened. But why were they also punished afterward for doing His will (Zechariah 1:15, 21)?

9. **Challenge question.** The elements of Zechariah's vision are very symbolic. It is stated in the text that the riders are angels. What do you think the horses represent? (You may want to compare this vision with a similar one in Revelation 6:1–8.)

Day 3 • Read Zechariah 2

10. In the vision, why would the man with the measuring line *not* need to determine the width and length of Jerusalem (vv. 4–5)?

11. Read Nehemiah 1:1–2:18.

a. Why was the wall of Jerusalem important to Nehemiah and the other people of Judah?

b. What do you think was indicated by the *lack* of a wall in Zechariah's vision?

12. In Zechariah 2:5, the Lord promises to be the glory in the midst of His people. Read Zephaniah 3:14–17; Matthew 1:23; 28:20; and John 1:14. How will the Lord dwell in the midst of His people?

13. Read Zechariah 2:10–11; Psalm 67; Isaiah 2:2–5; and Matthew 5:14.

a. What is God's plan for all of the Gentile nations?

b. When does this take place?

c. What is the role of a Christian in this plan?

Day 4 • Read Zechariah 3

14. Read Job 1:6–12; 2:1–10; Revelation 12:7–12.

a. Why is Satan described as an accuser?

b. For what purpose does God permit Satan to do this?

15. In Zechariah 3:3–5, what does Joshua's change of clothes signify for Christians? (Consider Isaiah 64:6 and Galatians 3:27.)

16. In Zechariah 3:2, the Lord rebukes Satan and describes Joshua the High Priest as being "a brand plucked from the fire." What does this description tell us about Joshua?

17. In Zechariah 3:8, there is a promise of the coming one called the Branch. Who is this Branch, and how does He fulfill the prophecy (Isaiah 4:2–4; 11:1–10; Jeremiah 23:5–6; 33:14–16)?

Day 5 • Read Zechariah 4

In this section of Zechariah, we see that the prophet has been given another highly symbolic vision. This one involves a lampstand and two olive trees.

18. a. What was the function of a lampstand in the tabernacle and temple? See Exodus 25:31–40 and 1 Kings 7:48–50.

b. Read Revelation 1:9–20. What does the lampstand signify in the New Testament?

19. In Zechariah's vision, what makes the lampstand burn perpetually without needing to be refilled with oil?

20. a. In Zechariah 4:12–14, the Lord identifies the two olive trees as symbolizing His two anointed ones. Who are these two anointed ones? Consider Leviticus 7:35–36 and 2 Samuel 2:4.

b. Who fulfills both of these anointed roles now? In other words, whom would the olive trees represent today? Consider Hebrews 7:26–27; John 18:36–37; and Matthew 28:18.

21. Review your answers for questions 19 and 20. What do you think it means that the New Testament lampstand will be forever fueled with oil from the olive trees?

Day 3 • Read Haggai 2:10–14

9. Read Leviticus 11 and Numbers 5:1–4. What made something clean or unclean?

10. Why was a dead body or carcass considered to be something that spreads uncleanness?

11. In Haggai 2:13–14, God compared the Israelites with a man who had been made unclean by touching a dead body. Everything that man touched would become unclean; likewise, everything the Israelites did was unclean. What does this description illustrate about the Israelites' spiritual condition?

12. Read Luke 10:30–37. The priest and the Levite may have been avoiding the injured man due to the risk of uncleanness that could be transferred to them from a dead body. The Samaritan, however, was not deterred by that concern. What do the actions of the Good Samaritan illustrate about the blessings we have in Jesus?

Day 4 • Read Haggai 2:15–19

13. What was Haggai's explanation for the lack of food and a poor yield from the people's vines and trees? (Consider also Haggai 1:2.)

14. "We walk by faith, not by sight" (2 Corinthians 5:7). What would make it especially difficult to believe this truth wholeheartedly at times?

15. Read Matthew 6:19–24. Evaluate Haggai's contemporaries in light of Jesus' words.

a. What treasure were they seeking?

b. What was destroying them?

c. How specifically could they lay up treasures in heaven?

16. Read James 1:1–18. How should a Christian face a time of trial? What is promised to the one who is faithful?

17. How would you respond to a suffering Christian who tells you, "I don't know why God is doing this to me"?

Day 5 • Read Haggai 2:20–23

18. A signet ring was a ring that had a unique impression on its surface. It would be pressed into the wet clay of a tablet to make an official mark or seal on the document. Such a seal carried the full authority of the person indicated by the mark. What do you think it means that Zerubbabel, the governor of Judah, was going to be made like a signet ring? (Also consider Matthew 1:13 and Colossians 1:15.)

19. Read Mark 13:1–8, 24–27. What does Jesus say is the purpose for the upheaval of "wars and rumors of wars" (v. 7)?

20. *For personal reflection. Sharing optional.* Read Psalm 91:1–10 and Romans 8:31–39. What promises comfort you during times when you see the world in upheaval?

21. Read Ephesians 6:10–20.

a. Even though Zerubbabel never fought a battle in Judah, in what way did he engage in warfare?

b. What weapons did God prepare for Zerubbabel (and also for you) with which to engage in this struggle?

12. Contrast the orders given in Haggai with the first temple building project (1 Kings 5:6–11; 6:14–38). Why do you think the Lord was not demanding that the people build an exact replica of Solomon's temple?

13. What was the deeper spiritual problem revealed by the Israelites building their homes while leaving the temple in disrepair?

14. Read Luke 12:13–21 and 14:15–24. What does it mean to be "rich toward God"? What does Jesus' parable of the great banquet teach us about the things we often value above Him?

15. *For personal reflection. Sharing optional.* Think about a time of great difficulty that forced you to rely more than before on your faith. What made that trial particularly effective in focusing your attention on God's mercy in Christ?

Day 4 • Read Haggai 1:12–13

16. Why are the "words of Haggai" equated with the "voice of the LORD" in verse 12?

17. What good news is present in the message "I am with you, declares the LORD"?

18. Read Romans 10:8–17 and Luke 10:16. How has God chosen to bring His Word near to us today?

19. What makes the Gospel preacher's feet beautiful (Romans 10:15)?

20. a. Why does the truth of "the one who hears you hears Me" (Luke 10:16) have the potential both to produce humility and to give rise to arrogance in the heart of the pastor?

b. How can a spirit of humility be encouraged?

Day 5 • Read Haggai 1:14–15

21. Read Exodus 35:20–36:2. What project was the Lord stirring up in the hearts of the people? What other similarities can you draw between this passage and Haggai 1?

22. Why were Cyrus and Darius uniquely qualified to give valuable assistance to the Israelites who were rebuilding the temple? See Ezra 1; Isaiah 44–45; and Ezra 6:1–12.

23. This prayer was written to be used during the Second Sunday in Advent to prepare for Christmas: "Stir up our hearts, O Lord, to make ready the way of Your only-begotten Son, that by His coming we may be enabled to serve You with pure minds; through the same Jesus Christ, our Lord, who lives and reigns with You and the Holy Spirit, one God, now and forever. Amen" (*LSB Altar Book*, pp. 555, 650, 745, 841). How does Haggai's message help prepare us for Christmas, as well as for Christ's final coming?

24. What does the Holy Spirit do in our hearts in order to motivate us to do God's will?

25. Read Acts 2:42–47.

a. What led the first Christian Church in Jerusalem to sell everything and distribute to anyone who had need?

b. Why would it be impossible to gain the same response in people by means of compulsion?

Day 3 • Selected Passages

When Cyrus rose to power in Persia, he decreed that the Israelite exiles could return to Jerusalem and rebuild the temple of the Lord. Today's readings will examine the importance of God's dwelling place with His people, first through the tabernacle and later the temple.

10. Read Numbers 2:1–2, 17. Where was the tabernacle (tent of meeting) located in relation to the rest of the Israelite tribes during their time of wandering in the wilderness? What do you think this arrangement symbolized?

11. a. Read 2 Samuel 7:1–17. What was David's desire for the Lord's dwelling place?

b. What did God promise instead when He refused David's request?

12. According to 1 Kings 6:12–13 and 9:3, how did Solomon's temple provide a vital link between God and the Israelites?

13. The temple rebuilt in Jerusalem after the Babylonian captivity was a smaller and less ornate structure than Solomon's temple. Nehemiah was the Israelite used by God to organize the rebuilding of the city walls.

a. Read Nehemiah 1:5–11. How did Nehemiah regard the (simpler) rebuilt temple?

b. Read Nehemiah 10:35–39. What obligations does he place on the people regarding the temple?

14. Though the temple was rebuilt in Nehemiah's time, and again by Herod the Great, it has never been rebuilt since its destruction in AD 70. Why is the physical temple in Jerusalem no longer necessary? Consider John 1:14, 17; 2:18–22; 6:19–20; Ephesians 2:17–22; and Hebrews 9:24–26.

Day 4 • Selected Passages

Both Zechariah and Malachi contain prophecies of the Last Day and the new creation—the final blessing of Christ's death and resurrection.

15. What blessings of the new creation belong to believers now? What is yet to come? Consider Isaiah 65:17–25 and Philippians 3:8–16.

16. Read Daniel 12:1–4. What are the main events of the Last Day? What does the book of names refer to? See Exodus 32:32–33 and Revelation 20:15; 21:27.

17. Read Matthew 25:31–46.

a. What is the evidence of saving faith that will be evident at the Last Judgment?

b. Why are both the righteous and the unrighteous not aware of their service or lack of service to Jesus?

18. When you face a difficulty, an illness, or the death of a loved one, what is it about the final coming of Christ that gives you the most comfort and spiritual healing?

Day 5 • Selected Passages

The end of Malachi's book begins a period of almost five hundred years between the last of the Old Testament books and the birth of Jesus. Today, we will consider the significance of this time after Haggai, Zechariah, and Malachi prophesied.

19. Before God called Samuel in 1 Samuel 3, it was said, "the word of the LORD was rare in those days; there was no frequent vision" (v. 1).

a. What do these phrases mean?

b. What was similar about the time between the Books of Malachi and Matthew?

20. It was Cyrus, King of Persia, who permitted the exiles to return to Jerusalem and rebuild the temple. As time passed, Persian dominance over Judah was replaced by the Greeks and then the Romans. With each change in overlord, the conditions of the people changed. This should not have been a surprise to the people, as it had happened to their forefathers when they were in Egypt. Read Exodus 1:6–12.

a. How did the history of Israel change when a new king arose in Egypt who did not know Joseph?

b. Keeping in mind the example of conditions in Egypt, how would you expect the situation to change for the people in Judah once the kings of Persia were no longer reigning over them?

c. **Challenge question.** If you were living in Judah at that time and knew that the final prophets (Zechariah and Malachi) had prophesied the coming of the Messiah to judge the world and reign over a purified, new creation, how would you consider life under Greek and Roman rule?

I Am Jesus' Little Lamb

The National Football League has teams named the Chicago Bears, Detroit Lions, Carolina Panthers, Denver Broncos, Atlanta Falcons, and St. Louis Rams. If the league ever expands to include new franchises, there will never be a team called the Los Angeles Lambs or the San Antonio Sheep. What would their cheerleaders say—"Fleece them, fleece them, baa, baa, baa"?

Sheep are not impressive creatures.

Zechariah also has a thing or two to say about sheep. "Strike the shepherd, and the sheep will be scattered" (Zechariah 13:7). The close relationship between the Lord and this Shepherd is indicated by the expression "the man who stands next to me" (v. 7). The Lord and His Shepherd stand side by side. They are equals. So why then does God call out, "Awake, O sword, against My shepherd" (v. 7)? What kind of relationship is this?

Sheep with a Shepherd

The Lord commands a sword to strike so sheep like us understand that our Shepherd's suffering and death were not accidental. Our Savior's death was no unexpected fluke. True, the events on Good Friday were simultaneously both an act of God and an act of people. Though this does not absolve from responsibility those who put Jesus to death, they were not in complete control of the situation. The disciples, Jewish leaders, and Romans did only what the Lord permitted them to do. He is the one who awakened the sword against the Shepherd.

In fact, the Father's plan for His Son was made before the creation of the world. At that time, He planned the birth of Judas, decided to create iron for nails that pierced our Savior's flesh, and conceived the idea of orchestrating events that led Pilate to Judea, Caiaphas to Jerusalem, and the crowds to repeatedly cry out, "Crucify Him, crucify Him!" This is what John means when he calls Him "the Lamb slain from the foundation of the world" (Revelation 13:8 NKJV).

When the Shepherd is struck, the sheep scatter. What else would we expect? Sheep are dumb. They graze on the same heights until the hills turn into desert wastes, polluted with disease. Sheep might even bend down to drink from a pond, get too close, allow the water to be absorbed into their wool, fall in, and drown! But we are not like that, are we?

Sheep are also dirty. Their wool is like a magnet. It attracts mud, manure, and maggots. It becomes caked with dirt, decay, and disease. Sheep absorb every particle of filth in the atmosphere. Of course, we aren't like that, are we?

And sheep are defenseless. They turn over on their back to rest but then are unable to get up. Canines, coyotes, and cougars all know that a cast sheep is a sitting duck! Surely you and I aren't like that, are we?

Hear the word of the Lord: "All we like sheep have gone astray; we have turned—every one—to his own way" (Isaiah 53:6).

Thank God that sheep like us have a Shepherd who leads His flock to find food on barren heights and gives unlimited water in the hottest of weather. He makes our path straight, compared with the normally hilly country where we are used to grazing. And our Shepherd tends to a large number of lambs that are drawn from great distances (49:9b–12).

Isaiah's Shepherd—indeed, Zechariah's Shepherd—is none other than Jesus Christ. His mission is singular: our Lord came to rescue, bind up, and bring home lost sheep (Matthew 9:36). He says, "I am the good shepherd. I know My own and My own know Me, just as the Father knows Me and I know the Father; and I lay down My life for the sheep" (John 10:14–15).

The pinnacle of our Shepherd's caring ministry was when, like a lamb, He was led to the slaughter (Isaiah 53:7). There were no green pastures; rather, spit and blood were caked on His cheeks. What about quiet waters? There was no water at all. That's why Jesus cried out, "I thirst" (John 19:28). His lips were cracked and swollen. His throat was parched from the hot Palestinian sun. Jesus passed through the valley of the shadow of death as it twanged its morbid melody. There was no rod or staff to comfort Him, only a spear to pierce His side. And the cup overflowed, all right; He drank from the cup of the fury of the wrath of God Almighty. Surely goodness and mercy were twisted and perverted in the most inhumane way. Reflecting on this great love, Peter writes, "He himself bore our sins in His body on the tree, that we might die to sin and live to righteousness. By His wounds you have been healed. For you were straying like sheep, but have now returned to the Shepherd and Overseer of your souls" (1 Peter 2:24–25).

Forever Led, Protected, Sustained

So often in our lives, we can feel as though we are completely alone. So often, as our troubles overwhelm us, we feel as though we have been rejected and cast off by God. Sometimes it seems as though we have no place to turn and that we have been left to fend for ourselves.

Yet, no matter how things may appear at those times, that is never the case. When you are lost and alone, your Shepherd leaves the ninety-nine and runs after you. When you are confused by the lies of demons and devils, He calls you by name, and you know that voice. When you are dirty and full of filth, He is the Lamb of God who takes away the sins of the world. Jesus is your Shepherd who gathers you in His arms until you are better, holds you until you can live with the hurt, and carries you close to His heart forever. And so we treasure the lyrics of this song, composed just for sheep like us.

I am Jesus' little lamb,
Ever glad at heart I am;
For my Shepherd gently guides me,
Knows my need and well provides me,
Loves me ev'ry day the same,
Even calls me by my name.

Day by day, at home, away,
Jesus is my staff and stay.
When I hunger, Jesus feeds me,
Into pleasant pastures leads me;
When I thirst, He bids me go
Where the quiet waters flow.

Who so happy as I am,
Even now the Shepherd's lamb?
And when my short life is ended,
By His angel host attended,
He shall fold me to His breast,
There within His arms to rest.
(*LSB* 740)

Portions of this article were adapted from "Savior of the Nations, Come," a series of Advent and Christmas sermons based on Isaiah 40:1–11, published by Concordia Seminary Press, 2011. Used with permission.

HOLY TO THE LORD

Zechariah ends his book with a vision of perfect holiness where even the bells on horses and mundane cooking utensils are made "holy to the Lord" (Zechariah 14:20–21). The description "holy to the Lord" recalls the same inscription upon the high priest's turban (Exodus 28:36–38). This designation is also applied to sacrifices offered or dedicated to the Lord (Leviticus 23:20), silver and gold vessels used in the temple (Ezra 8:28), and the spoils of holy war (Joshua 6:19).

Excluded, though, from this holiness is the "trader." This is how the KJV, NRSV, and ESV sometimes translate the Hebrew term "Canaanite." Although "Canaanite" can refer to a merchant or trader, in Zechariah 14:21 it is better to transliterate the Hebrew and render the word "Canaanite." Why? Because God has nothing against those who buy and sell in the marketplace; He has everything against pagan Canaanites.

Approaching the Holy One

The transgression of Noah's son Ham, whose son was Canaan (Genesis 9:20–25), launched a line of people whose sin and sexual depravity grieved the Lord. Canaanites polluted the Promised Land with their idolatry and immoral lifestyles. Zechariah uses the term "Canaanite" in this context, not to refer to a specific nationality, but to denote unbelievers whose lives demonstrated the opposite of God's holiness.

Zechariah derives his vision of holiness from ideas first expressed in the Book of Exodus. The plan to make everything holy was first launched when God appeared to Moses in the burning bush. The Lord came down to rescue Israel and appeared on holy ground. His presence first unleashed the plagues against the Egyptians and then settled upon Mount Sinai, where for forty days He gave instructions to Moses.

However, God wanted to dwell with the Israelites in a permanent way, so He told Moses, "And let [the Israelites] make Me a sanctuary [the Hebrew is *miqdash*, meaning "holy place"], that I may dwell in their midst" (Exodus 25:8). The sanctuary was to bring heaven to earth and allow the Lord to take up residency among His people. So the Israelites diligently built the sanctuary.

This sanctuary, or tabernacle, was designed to have different levels of holiness. Concerning the metals, the posts holding up the courtyard curtain were silver hooks and rings (27:10–11). The frames that constituted the sidewalls were silver (26:19–21). Inside the tabernacle, most of the furnishings and appointments were pure gold. Regarding levels of access, Gentiles and unclean Israelites lived outside the camp. Israelites dwelled inside the camp, while only Levites encamped in the immediate vicinity of the tabernacle. The high priest alone had access to the Most Holy Place once a year to make atonement for sin. The curtains also demonstrate these different layers (vv. 1–14). The outermost curtains were fine goatskin leather. The innermost curtains were made out of "blue and purple and scarlet yarns; you shall make them with cherubim skillfully worked into them" (v. 1).

Once all of this was in place, God descended from Mount Sinai and entered the sanctuary. "And Moses was not able to enter the tent of meeting because the cloud settled on it, and the glory of the Lord filled the tabernacle" (40:35). No one was able to enter the tabernacle, not even Moses! Thus, the Book of Exodus ends with a paradox: God resides on earth, but people are unable to access the forgiving power of His holiness.

The ordination of priests is God's solution to this problem. The Lord separates out a group, Aaron and his sons, to work within the sanctuary and to mediate His real presence to the people through sacred rites. The office of the priest is described

in Exodus 28–30, but the ordination rite does not take place until Leviticus 8–9.

Israel's priesthood, though, derives from the fact that the entire nation was "a kingdom of priests and a holy nation" (Exodus 19:6). The Book of Exodus proclaims that God's election of Israel, far from meaning the rejection of others, is the very means of salvation for the nations. This "holy nation" sets apart some of its members to be priests to administer the Lord's forgiving presence so that they, in turn, could be the channel and conduit of this grace for the world. The covenant at Sinai reiterates the commission given to Abraham: "I will make of you a great nation, and I will bless you, and make your name great, and you, be a blessing. I will bless those who bless you, and the one who curses you I will curse; and in you all the families of the earth shall be blessed" (Genesis 12:2–3, author's translation).

The flow of thought in Exodus 19:5–6 therefore runs like this: "Listen to My voice and do what I command, and in so doing, you shall show yourselves to be My people and as for My part, I will be your God and perform the oath sworn to the ancestors. The nations will see this relationship, and by faith some will become a part of My chosen people."

The Lord's goal is neither for His holy presence to remain confined to a sanctuary, nor that its transformative power be restricted to an ordained class of priests. He wants all Israelites to receive holiness and then to become holy themselves. God's broader intention is reinforced with the additional divine proclamation "All the earth is Mine" (Exodus 19:5). The Lord's universal rule is the setting in which the holiness of the nation is meant to function. The people of God were empowered to take the role of priests for the sake of the world. Likewise we, as the people of God in this New Testament era, are also empowered as priests for the same purpose: to proclaim the wonder of the holy God to a fallen world.

The Coming Kingdom of Holiness

However, Israel, more often than not, failed in their calling. Despising the holiness of God, they preferred the immorality of Canaan and so failed to proclaim the holiness of God, not just to the world, but even to themselves.

We are called, just like Israel, "to proclaim the mighty acts of Him who called you out of darkness into His marvelous light" (1 Peter 2:9, author's translation). You and I have the privilege of inviting people to share in God's coming kingdom, where everything will be beautiful, perfect, and holy, just as Zechariah describes it. The vision of holiness will be a promise no longer, for it will have found its fulfillment in Christ. The holiness of God will then be fully revealed and fully enjoyed by all who are in Christ Jesus, even forever.

Who's Who in the

© Shutterstock, Inc.

Book of Zechariah

Zechariah introduces us to a wide variety of people that we probably don't know too much about. It would be so easy for us to simply read over the names, ignore them, and just keep on reading. But by doing that, we would be missing so much of this amazing book of prophecy. Learning about some of the significant people in the book will help us better understand and appreciate the dramatic oracles given by God to Zechariah.

DARIUS THE KING

Public Domain

Let's begin with Darius, the first person Zechariah mentions in his book. It is important to note that the only three dates the prophet mentions all include Darius, Persia's king from 522–486 BC.

Like Cyrus the Great, the founder of the Persian Empire, Darius allowed his subjects a vast amount of freedom. In contrast to the Assyrians and Babylonians—who were notorious for their brutality—Persia allowed and even encouraged conquered nations to develop their own life and to maintain their traditions. Darius codified local laws and organized his empire into twenty satrapies. Satrapies, or protectorates, were Persia's largest administrative units. God's people in Judah were part of the satrapy called "Beyond the River."

During Darius's rule, Persia reached the summit of its material power, the height of its economic prosperity, and the pinnacle of its territorial expansion. At the same time, the empire became famous for its support of local religions. For example, Darius continued Cyrus's policy of paying for the building of temples (Ezra 6:8). He also asked, once the temple was rebuilt, for the people of Judah to daily pray for him and his children (v. 10).

JOSHUA THE HIGH PRIEST

Public Domain

Joshua the high priest worked together with Judah's governor Zerubbabel. In fact, in one of Zechariah's visions, two olive trees symbolize Zerubbabel and Joshua (Zechariah 4:3, 7). The oracle announces that God's blessings will come through the community's two leaders. Priest and governor will stand side by side, like two pillars upon which the Lord will build His kingdom.

Both Haggai and Zechariah indicate that Joshua's father was Jehozadak. This connects Joshua to the lineage of Seraiah the high priest who was executed by the Babylonians at Riblah (see 1 Chronicles 6:14–15 and 2 Kings 25:18–21). Seraiah's son, Jehozadak, was exiled to Babylon, and it was there that Joshua was born.

In the prophet's fourth vision, Zechariah sees Joshua clothed with filthy garments and being arraigned before the heavenly tribunal. Satan stands at Joshua's side, ready to denounce him. Why was the high priest guilty? Perhaps since Joshua was born in Babylon, an unclean land, he was disqualified from serving as priest. After all, God had earlier spurned Eli's priesthood (see 1 Samuel 2:27–33). Why couldn't He do the same with Joshua? However, the Lord silences Satan before charges are brought. Joshua's filthy garments are taken off, and God announces that his iniquity is forgiven. A clean turban is placed on his head and he is clothed with new garments. Joshua is consecrated as high priest, and his powers are expanded to include administrative and judicial functions.

ZECHARIAH THE PROPHET

© IStockphoto.com

Zechariah means "the Lord remembered." Twenty-nine people go by this name in the Old Testament; two of whom, in addition to the prophet, lived during postexilic times. Therefore, to avoid confusion, Zechariah the prophet states that he is "the son of Berechiah, son of Iddo" (Zechariah 1:1). His ministry overlapped Haggai's by a month, and it seems likely that these prophets were aware of each other's ministries. For instance, Zechariah 8 echoes many of the motifs proclaimed in Haggai 1. Furthermore, both of these prophets envision a community where God's appointed leaders, Zerubbabel and Joshua, govern His people in ways of peace and prosperity.

Zechariah encouraged the people to finish the temple, while also helping them transition from being an independent kingdom ruled by David and his successors to being under Persian control that only allowed a governor. The prophet's greatness was his ability to lead God's people who were initially too busy with their own concerns to concentrate on rebuilding the temple. Zechariah enabled the faithful remnant to pick up the pieces of the exile and embrace God's promises that would come to fruition in Christ Jesus.

ZERUBBABEL THE GOVERNOR

Public Domain

Zerubbabel is called Judah's governor in Haggai, though he is not described this way in the Book of Zechariah. His position of leadership was most likely a consequence of his direct descent from David through Jehoiakim, one of the last kings of Judah (see 1 Chronicles 3:16–17 and Matthew 1:11–12).

Zerubbabel oversaw a remnant community that was beset by opposition from the outside and discouragement from within. The chief problem, though, was that construction on the second temple had stalled. Compared with Solomon's temple, this building was far less impressive. No wonder Zechariah, in chapter 4, reminded the governor not to despise small beginnings! The prophet encouraged him to not grow weary while rebuilding the temple. Any obstacles in Zerubbabel's way would be removed and the governor would bring the work to its completion through God's Spirit.

Whereas Haggai states that Zerubbabel's father was named Shealtiel, nowhere in his book does Zechariah mention this. What are we to make of this? It seems that Zechariah wants to downplay Zerubbabel's descent from King David so as not to incite unrealistic hope in imminent restoration of the monarchy. At the same time, the prophet makes it clear that the current configuration was only temporary—God's ultimate plan would materialize through the rule of Jesus our Lord.

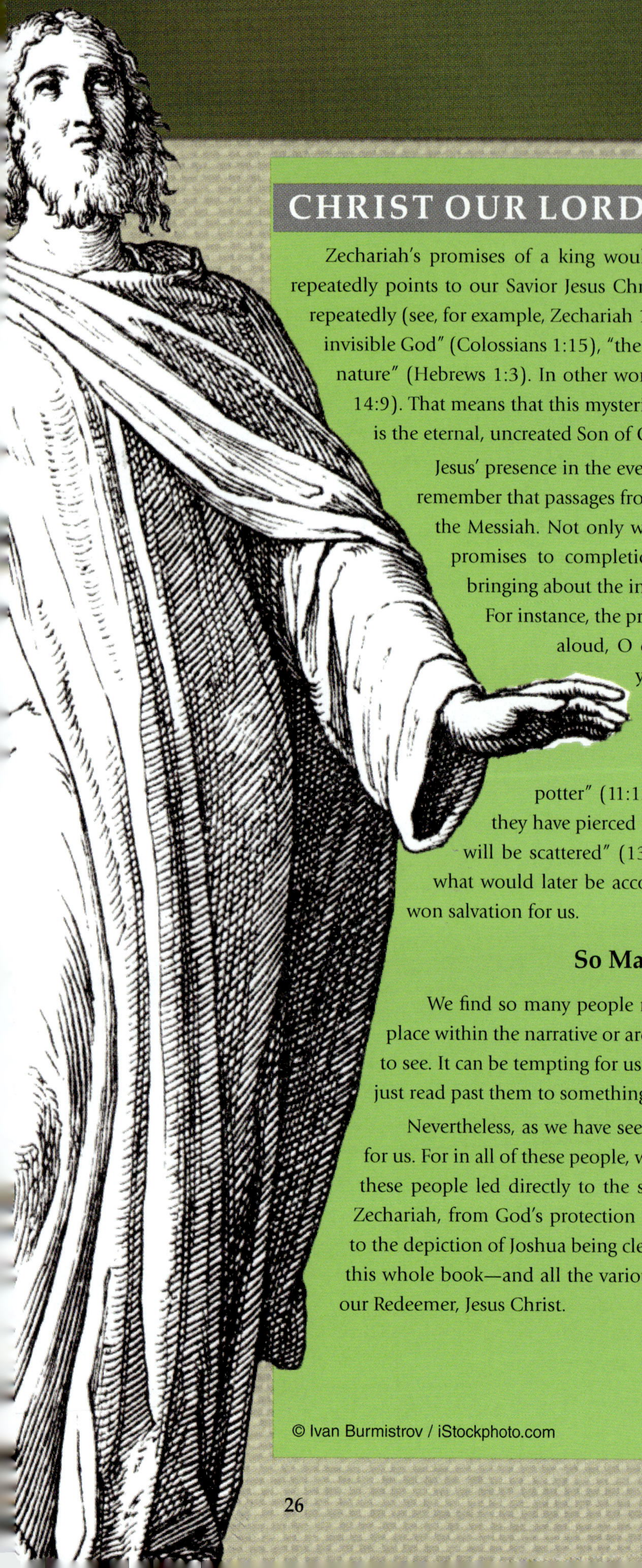

CHRIST OUR LORD

Zechariah's promises of a king would most certainly come to pass. This is why his book repeatedly points to our Savior Jesus Christ, chiefly through the Angel of the Lord who appears repeatedly (see, for example, Zechariah 1:9–14). In New Testament terms, "He is the image of the invisible God" (Colossians 1:15), "the radiance of the glory of God and the exact imprint of His nature" (Hebrews 1:3). In other words, anyone who sees this "Angel" sees the Father (John 14:9). That means that this mysterious being is not merely some created angel, but that He is the eternal, uncreated Son of God. This "Angel of the Lord" is actually Jesus!

Jesus' presence in the events of this book should not be at all surprising when we remember that passages from Zechariah 9–14 are full of God's promises concerning the Messiah. Not only was our Lord Christ present and active in bringing these promises to completion centuries later, but He was present and active in bringing about the initial proclamation of these promises through Zechariah. For instance, the prophet writes, "Rejoice greatly, O daughter of Zion! Shout aloud, O daughter of Jerusalem! Behold, your king is coming to you; righteous and having salvation is He, humble and mounted on a donkey, on a colt, the foal of a donkey" (9:9). Again he says, "So I took the thirty pieces of silver and threw them into the house of the LORD, to the potter" (11:13). And again, "When they look on Me, on Him whom they have pierced . . ." (12:10). Finally, "Strike the shepherd, and the sheep will be scattered" (13:7). With breathtaking detail, these oracles prophesied what would later be accomplished during Holy Week and how Christ our Lord won salvation for us.

So Many People, So Much Grace

We find so many people referred to in the Book of Zechariah. They either have a place within the narrative or are depicted in the various visions that the prophet is given to see. It can be tempting for us to simply ignore these references as being irrelevant and just read past them to something that may not seem quite so obscure.

Nevertheless, as we have seen, the various references to people are highly significant for us. For in all of these people, we see the grace of God at work as the events surrounding these people led directly to the salvation we receive in Christ. All through the Book of Zechariah, from God's protection of His people under the rule of an unbelieving Persian, to the depiction of Joshua being cleansed of his sins, to the images of our Lord's crucifixion, this whole book—and all the various people mentioned in the book—points us directly to our Redeemer, Jesus Christ.

Malachi and Money Management

What subject is likely to send temperatures boiling around the American home? Is it politics? Not even in the running. Is it sex? the in-laws? These issues are often contested, but they are not on the front burner. The answer is money. *Money* is the number one fighting word in the American family.

Money deludes us into thinking that it can give us ultimate security and happiness, yet all the while it is the very source of our greatest worries. If our hearts are set only on money, our reward is an anxiety whose burden sooner or later destroys us.

Financial worries are unnatural. "Look at the birds of the air: they neither sow nor reap nor gather into barns, and yet your heavenly Father feeds them. Are you not of more value than they?" (Matthew 6:26). Apprehension about savings, bank accounts, retirement plans, the stock market, and the like is also unhelpful. "And which of you by being anxious can add a single hour to his span of life?" (v. 27). And obsessing about money is unbelieving. "Therefore do not be anxious, saying, 'What shall we eat?' or 'What shall we drink?' or 'What shall we wear?' For the Gentiles seek after all these things, and your heavenly Father knows that you need them all" (vv. 1–32). The verdict is in. Either we manage money, or money will manage us!

The Myth of "More"

Thank God the prophet Malachi has something to say about money. He begins with these words from the Lord: "I have loved you" (Malachi 1:2a). Our God has a deep, abiding affection for us! God's eternal love and His deep tenderness for us are the only foundation for liberating money management.

The problem, though, was that the people Malachi addressed had bought in to the myth of "more." The lie goes something like this: "Having more money and more things will make me more important, more significant, and more secure. So I must spend my life getting more and more!" This is why the people of Judah were bringing the Lord blind, injured, crippled, blemished, and diseased animals for sacrifice (vv. 8, 13, 14). They were saving the best of the flock for themselves. The people wanted more for themselves and less for everyone else, including God.

Early in my marriage, our furniture style was "Late Garage Sale." So one day I splurged. Right after my spending spree, my wife and I visited a church member's house. On our way home, I remarked, "Wow, Lisa, did you see that furniture? It goes back to Louis the Fourteenth." To which she replied, "Right, and if you don't make our payments, ours goes back to Sears on the fifteenth!"

Our yearning for more brings with it high levels of debt, despair, and depression. Left unchecked, it will drive a stake into every relationship we have.

True Contentment

How can we deal with our titanic desire to acquire? How can the words of the apostle Paul be true in our life: "I have learned in whatever situation I am to be content" (Philippians 4:11)? And just how do we live in a society that tells us daily to buy things we don't need with money we don't have to impress people we don't even like?

Malachi provides the solution. He writes these words: "Bring the full tithe into the storehouse, that there may be food in My house. And thereby put Me to the test, says the Lord of hosts, if I will not open the windows of heaven for you and pour down for you a blessing until there is no more need" (Malachi 3:10). The tithe was the dedication of a tenth of a person's produce or livestock. It was first commanded in Leviticus 27:30–31 and functioned primarily as a means to support the priests and Levites. Through Malachi, the Lord describes His unchangeable love and urges the people to break the myth of "more" by returning a portion of their income to Him. In doing so, they will find a new freedom.

What does this look like, though, in practical ways? First, give to the Lord. "Honor the Lord with your wealth and with the firstfruits of all your produce" (Proverbs 3:9). You and I make a living by what we get; we make a life by what we give. So first and foremost, give generously and cheerfully to the Lord and His Church. Second, give to yourself. That's right. There is nothing wrong about giving to yourself, once you've given sacrificially to God. "Wealth gained hastily will dwindle, but whoever gathers little by little will increase it" (13:11). It is a godly thing to save, invest, and plan for the future. Third, give to others. "The wicked borrows but does not pay back, but the righteous is generous and gives" (Psalm 37:21). Don't be a miser when it comes to charities and causes that promote the Gospel of Christ. *Miser*, after all, makes up the word *miserable*. I've never met a happy tightwad.

Why follow this money management plan? In Malachi 3:17, the Lord calls us His "treasured possession." This title originally applied to all Israel (Exodus 19:5), but now this little group of Judah's descendants in the insignificant Persian province of Yehud in the fifth century BC receives the same designation! Used only eight times in the Old Testament, the words refer to a prized, priceless possession.

Money deludes us into thinking that it can give us ultimate security and happiness, yet all the while, it is the very source of our greatest worries. If our hearts are set only on money, our reward is an anxiety whose burden sooner or later destroys us.

From the depths of His loving heart, God beams over each of us and says, "I have redeemed you; I have called you by name, you are Mine" (Isaiah 43:1). This baptismal gift fully cleanses and forgives. With water and the Word, the Father placed His mark of ownership upon us: "Receive the sign of the holy cross both upon your forehead and upon your heart to mark you as one redeemed by Christ the crucified" (*LSB*, p. 268).

The Strongest of All Desires

We all struggle at times with the myth of "more." We all are tempted at times to withhold from God so that we can have more for ourselves. We all are tempted with that burning desire to acquire. Yet, in these things, we never do find the contentment we were seeking.

Even stronger than our grasping desires is God's desire for us. Because we are redeemed by Jesus, true contentment in life may always be found, even if we can't always have "more." Trusting in Christ, you have your most precious possession and your heart's greatest desire: the unconditional and never-failing love of God.

Galileo
was wrong,
The universe does
revolve around me

Turning Our Hearts Toward Home

Some time ago a clothing ad appeared that contained a picture of several T-shirts. Emblazoned across the front of one of the shirts was this statement: "I'm my own role model."

This brazen preoccupation with self is the driving force of American culture. "Self-" has become the modifier of choice. Common are the terms: *self-image, self-esteem, self-actualization, self-understanding, self-acceptance, self-expression, self-fulfillment, self-concept,* and *self-help*. Big hit movies in recent years like *Star Wars* and *Raiders of the Lost Ark* contain the same plot: *one person* against either Darth and the Dark Empire or Nazi Germany. The story lines come down to this: a lone individual relies on self and single-handedly saves the day. It is the story that shapes our dreams and defines our hopes. Whom do we admire? Luke Skywalker, Indiana Jones, and *ourselves*. A slogan on another T-shirt sums up where we are: "Galileo was wrong. The universe *does* revolve around me."

This brazen preoccupation with **SELF** is the driving force of American culture.

This fascination with self has wreaked havoc on the American family. Homes are discordant and disjointed. Tearing at their foundation are rising divorce rates, out-of-wedlock births, parental abandonment, teen suicide, homosexual rights, and the list goes on and on.

Malachi turns our hearts toward home. Some of his last words promise that God's plan includes turning "the hearts of fathers to their children and the hearts of children to their fathers" (Malachi 4:6). A strong sense of community pervaded Israelite households. In the Old Testament, fulfillment in life, to use a modern term, was not achieved individualistically, as, for example, through personal adventure or professional achievement. Nor was it corporate in the context of some larger community overriding the familial structures, such as citizenship in a state. It meant, instead, to be embedded in the texture of the generations and to participate harmoniously as a member of a family. This was life with a promise and a future.

Life with a Promise and a Future

Most Israelite households were multigenerational, consisting of two or three families related by kinship and marriage, living in a residential complex of two or three houses connected together. Solidarity continued as deceased members were commemorated as an essential component of this organic whole. This is noted by means of the frequent reference to be "gathered to [one's] fathers" (for example, Judges 2:10) or "gathered to [one's] people" (Genesis 25:8).

It followed that the cardinal sin, the sin that lay at the root of all sin, was whatever bound Israelites to impersonal or anti-personal existence. Sin was the denial that people were created, redeemed, and sanctified to be in relationship with others, beginning with the family.

The Hebrews had no love of isolation. Indeed, to be alone meant that something unusual or threatening was happening. Psalm 25:15–16 states, "My eyes are ever toward the Lord, for He will pluck my feet out of the net. Turn to me and be gracious to me, for I am lonely and afflicted." Being alone as a longed-for benefit that gives pleasure is alien to the Old Testament. The sense of identity and self-awareness of the individual living in a network of social relations was significantly different from those of the typical privatized individual of western, post-industrial, urban society. The segregated person is easily overcome. God's remedy for the problem of being alone is the family: "God settles the solitary in a home" (68:6).

Not only did the social and economic realms converge on the family, but so did the spiritual. One example is in Judges 2:10: "And all that generation also were gathered to their fathers. And there arose another generation after them who did not know the Lord or the work that He had done for Israel." The failure of parents to tell their children the mighty acts of God had serious repercussions. The next generation served Canaanite fertility gods and goddesses, and the land was attacked. Israel understood that its religious ideas as set forth by the Lord were largely carried out in relationship with members of their home.

The stellar example of how family solidarity was displayed in Israel is seen in the institution of the "kinsman-redeemer." He was the next of kin responsible for the justice and well-being of the family. His responsibilities were fourfold. First, he avenged the murder of a kinsperson (Numbers 35:16–21). Second, he maintained the family's ownership of its inheritance (Deuteronomy 25:5–10). This practice of levirate marriage (from the Latin term *levir*, meaning "brother-in-law"), in which the next of kin, generally the brother, married the widow in order to raise legal descendants to inherit the estate of her childless dead husband, also served to keep the family intact. Third, he secured a kinsperson's release from debt. Fourth, he redeemed family members in debt. These duties included providing interest-free loans, making sure the needy relative didn't become a slave, and redeeming them from slavery if the poor relative or his dependents had sold themselves to an outsider (Leviticus 25:23–55).

Solidarity made the Israelite family the basic unit of society rather than the individual. Solidarity kept the integrity and the dignity of male-female roles and parent-child roles in a more holistic perspective. It also included respecting the older generation. Beyond that, it also highlighted the relational emphasis of the best virtues in the Old Testament: loyalty, sacrifice, love, long-suffering, mercy, commitment, and forgiveness.

The Way the Universe Revolves

Against any temptation to sing Frank Sinatra's "I did it my way," the Old Testament refused to view people in light of self-service and self-absorption. Israelites maintained that personal existence is constituted by relationships with other people. "I" am constituted as a person only in reference to "you." The focus is on the other, not on the self.

God's love in Jesus Christ empowers family solidarity where husbands and wives, parents and children, grandparents, cousins, aunts and uncles live out honest and caring relationships that are mutually interdependent. By means of the Old Testament, families are provided the blueprint needed to be strong, supportive, and spiritual institutions. Joshua's words at Shechem are the prophetic voice that needs to be heard anew: "As for me and my house, we will serve the Lord" (Joshua 24:15).

Galileo was *right*. The universe does not revolve around me. It revolves around the Lord and the people He places into my family.